THE JET PROGRAM AND YOU

Your guide to survival as a JET

Table of Contents

Before you read this book

This book is for everyone. Whether you've been teaching in Japan for a year and you need advice, or you've just found out you made the cut and aren't sure what to pack, or maybe you're on the verge of applying and need some pointers, this book is here to serve you. I hope this book will inspire you to pursue a job in the JET Program, but also understand that the program isn't a vacation. Some of the topics discussed in this E-book are sensitive due to cultural misconceptions and sharing personal stories myself and other JETs experienced.

I hope this book will help you make the most of your JET experience and help you overcome some problems you could face in the classroom and living in a foreign country. If you have any questions my email is at the end of the book and I'm more than happy to help.

Please note that all of the student and faculty names mentioned in this book have been changed with the exception of known companies such as MSI Japan and MacMillan Publishing.

Happy reading and good luck!

Introduction

You've finally decided to take the plunge to live abroad and teach in Japan. Good for you! Not many people in the world can do what you're trying to do, and I guarantee you're in for a life-changing experience. Japan has been a large part of my life. I've been traveling back and forth between Japan and the U.S. since 2011 and my collective experience reached a total of three years and two months in the country as of 2017. Being exposed to a different culture outside of the United States and having the opportunity to live there truly changed my perspective on life in a positive way, and as I write this, I hope living in Japan will provide you the same outcome.

The Japan Exchange and Teaching Program (JET) is a great way to kick off your career while being exposed to a different culture, lifestyle and way of thinking. It all began in 1987, when the JET program was founded with the hope of increasing mutual understanding between Japan and the outside world through language learning and cross-cultural events. Since its founding, the JET program has grown from an average of 800 participants to over 5000 going to Japan each year with the hope of contributing to international peace and cross-cultural development.

I won't lie. The competition for this prestigious program is steep with only 20% of all U.S. applicants being accepted. The JET Program receives an average of 4,000 to 5,000 applications from the U.S. and of these around 1,000 will be chosen. Although the U.S.A. holds a large quantity of the total possible seats, several countries send JETs to the program. Most of the participants in the JET program are called Assistant Language Teachers (ALTs), followed by Coordinators of International Relations (CIRs), and once in a blue moon, Sports Exchange Advisors (SEAs). I'll touch upon these positions in the application portion of this book, but here is a quick sheet on the acceptance numbers from last year as of July 1st 2017.

Country	ALTs accepted	CIRs accepted	SEAs accepted	Total Accepted
U.S.A.	1,015	43	1	1,059
Canada	171	10	0	181

United Kingdom	142	12	0	154
Australia	127	4	0	131
New Zealand	77	5	0	82

For a more detailed chart including additional countries and information for first and 5th years, check http://jetprogramme.org/en/countries/

On top of the competition, the application process is a bit of an emotional roller coaster, with lots of tasks you'll have to fulfill from autumn to late spring. The JET Program is like a marathon that requires you to pace yourself and keep up with deadlines, while also causing you to secure other job possibilities in the event you don't make it. If you keep up with all of the deadlines and you are well received in your essay and interview, the real fun begins abroad. But even then, there will be challenges in the classroom, in society, and within you. You're going to change and grow as a person as you navigate your way in a new work environment. Some of these issues you can solve with the help of the Board of Education and your fellow JETs, but others not so much. The Board of Education in Japan is often times reluctant to address some of the more sensitive topics, which is where I come in. My goals for this guide are three-fold:

1. To give you a leg up on the competition.

2. Provide you a smooth transition into life in Japan.

3. Help you solve some of the many problems you may encounter.

If all goes according to plan, you'll be able to open up this book for a quick and detailed answer when you run into trouble or if you have a question. Let's begin!

Matsue castle. I highly recommend you visit Sakai Minato

if you get the chance.

Chapter 1: Is JET Right For You? The Application Process

Is the JET Program right for you?

Before we dive into the application and the types of questions you might be asked and how you might best present yourself, we need to answer the most important question: "Is the JET Program right for you?" I'm assuming that you've already given the JET Program some thought before applying and that you've set your sights on it, but I'd like you to consider these questions before writing your application.

1) *Are you willing to look past any assumptions you have about the JET Program?*

   The famous quote that JET likes to throw around is "Everyone's experience is different." This means you could be living in a home with a hole in the ceiling exposed to the elements in the countryside of Shikoku, or you might be in the flashing city lights of Tokyo, one of the newer locations in the program. You might be placed in a school that sets really high expectations of you from day one, or you might be left to your own devices in the teacher's room. Your experience could be very different from that of your neighbor who just returned from the JET Program three months ago. My point is to ask yourself: "Are you willing to craft your own experiences and adapt to situations?"

2) *Can you devote at least one year of your time to living abroad and working as a professional in a Japanese work environment?*

   For many people this is a no-brainer, but the fact is Japan is known for its demanding work schedules, strict guidelines, desire for perfection and constant improvement. Also, please keep in mind that the JET Program is not a way to climb up the career ladder. There is no promotion with rewards, and while you're abroad, your world back home will continue to move. People you know get married, relatives pass away, friends climb up in the workplace ladder and develop lucrative careers. As you watch this from afar on social media, you can't say suddenly "I want to go home, I've had enough of this vacation. Bye!" The JET Program doesn't work that way.

Due to the application timeline, the different schedule of the school year and the difficulty of finding replacement teachers and especially CIRs, you are obligated to provide not one month's notice, but rather several. There will be things you miss while you're abroad, and if you can live with yourself despite missing out on some of these experiences, carry on.

3) *Are you willing to work towards peaceful resolutions to problems and be a cultural bridge between your country and Japan?*

Let me say frankly, culture differences can be great, but they can also be a royal pain in the butt. What you may think is okay in your home country might not be suitable in Japan and vice versa. The important thing for you is to put yourself out there, give new experiences a try and don't be judgmental. When a mistake or misunderstanding occurs, find a solution to it in a way both parties understand what happened and why it happened. In our day and age, cultural differences can lead to harsh exchanges of words and even war, but most of the time cultural differences and cooperative understanding can lead to great friendships and stories you can share for the rest of your life. If you can stay positive no matter what is thrown at you and be optimistic, then keep reading.

Asking these questions seriously before you apply is an important step since you might need to have some discussions with family, friends, and loved ones. Consider your options, outcomes, and opportunities and dive in if you're excited. These questions might even help you prepare for your interview, so being able to talk openly about them will give you an advantage as you prepare for an interesting stage of your life.

The application

For the sake of simplicity, I will be discussing the process from the American point of view and my own experiences. If you're living outside of the United States, please confirm the application due dates and process with your JET program representatives in your home country and visit the appropriate website. The exact dates change each year, so it will be your responsibility to keep track of each deadline of the application and submit your documents on time.

From what I understand after studying the JET application for several years online and the recent 2018 application, the application process typically begins in late September. You will have anywhere from four to five weeks to get everything filled out and submitted. The JET Program website should have a signup list where you can provide your email to stay in the loop for application dates. Be aware though, there is a chance for the email from the website to go into your spam folders, so try to mark it so any future emails will go to your primary inbox. Lastly, don't forget to check the Jet Program website daily for updates and news.

As you're waiting for the application window to open up, you might be wondering: "what can I do before the application process even begins to get a leg up on the competition?" For you college seniors, I recommend coming up with three professors you could talk to and confidently ask for a letter of recommendation into the program. Don't approach them yet, but just keep them in mind. If you're taking their classes, try to get good grades or put in a lot of effort. Play the game and get those teachers on your side.

For those of you in graduate school, definitely ask your thesis advisor for a letter of recommendation. Not asking would be insulting, especially if they find out you got in and didn't even consider them worthy of asking for help when they're already helping you graduate with an advanced degree. Old professors from your bachelor's degree are acceptable, but try to limit it to only one if possible. If you're out of college and in the workforce, you can ask for two reference letters from higher-ups if you find it difficult to get a recent recommendation letter from your university.

Remember, just keep a list of names in mind for when the application period opens and be prepared to provide backups. I remember when I requested a letter of recommendation from my language school instructor in Tokyo and although she intended to write me one, she was unable to. In the final weeks of the application she had to take her child to the hospital, attend a funeral and then a wedding. I only had a little bit of time left to collect a backup recommender and my list of people saved me. Life just takes over sometimes, so it is best to be prepared for the worst-case scenario.

Once the application period opens you will have four to five weeks to get everything prepared. A standard application package includes:

Mandatory forms
- General application form
- Self-assessment medical form
- University transcripts
- Degree or proof of expected graduation
- Statement of purpose
- Two reference letters
- Proof of American citizenship

Additional forms depending on whether you meet certain criteria:
- Physicians form
- Proof of teacher's certification
- Proof of TEFL / TESL qualification
- Proof of Japanese proficiency
- FBI background check result
- Certificate of health

General application form and positions

This is your typical form where it will ask you for your current education or employment position, address, employment history and other basic information. The most important thing to consider at this stage is what kind of job do you want? If you want to be an Assistant Language Teacher (ALT), you'll be primarily teaching in a classroom with a range from children to adults in an urban or country setting. If you like working with different age groups and want the traditional JET experience most people have, this is the job for you. A Coordinator for International Relations (CIR) will involve an even broader range of activities, from translating documents from Japanese to English or even vice versa. Depending on your language skills you may be interpreting at events, providing tours, planning international exchange programs, writing for the local newspaper, and teaching at school a few times a week though you will mainly work in your region's city hall. The CIR in my opinion is a more language-demanding job and is great if you want to put your skills to the test and want a career in international relations, media, event hosting, or management. However, the number of CIR positions available is limited and will vary each year depending on whether a slot opens up. The final position is the Sports

Exchange Advisor (SEA). This is an extremely rare position where the individual will work with local governments to promote international exchange through sports. It's a fun and demanding job, but the recruitment process is vastly different since an applicant must be recommended by their home country's National Olympic Committee or a government organization.

HEADS UP: If you apply as a CIR and pass the interview and there happens to be more qualified CIR applicants than positions available, you may be given the chance to switch over to an ALT provided you have relevant experience to be an ALT and give consent. You will be notified if this does happen. Be prepared to discuss why you chose to be an ALT or CIR in your interview since many JETs I know who had high language skills were questioned why they applied to be an ALT rather than a CIR.

Rumor bash: I've heard previous JETs, current JETs, bloggers, and aspiring JETs state that the JET Program doesn't want ALTs who know Japanese or anyone who doesn't know a single word of Japanese or has teaching experience. Some go as far to claim that the JET Program is one big political conspiracy with the hope of promoting false English education by hiring ill-trained and insufficient staff lacking basic Japanese communication skills. I'm going to put this to rest and say these people have no idea what they're talking about. Ignore the angry forum posts on Reddit. They're not going to help you.

The JET program committee chooses whomever they feel will contribute to the program and best represent their home country abroad in a professional manner. While having language skills and teaching experience is a plus, it will not guarantee your position if you act like a jerk during the interview or if you lie in your application. After all, being a JET is more than being a teacher or a translator. Your job is to expose the Japanese to a different way of thinking and culture. So, if you're wondering as to whether or not you should hide something in your application, DON'T! Consider any teaching experience and language experience as icing on the cake to your application. If you claim to speak Japanese on paper, be prepared to speak in your oral interview. I can't tell you how many times I've heard horror stories of people saying they got caught lying since they couldn't say anything besides "hello" in Japanese despite claiming they could speak fluently when they were applying for an ALT position. Don't be that person!

Self-assessment medical form

For the medical form you don't need a doctor or primary physician's signature. This is your own quick assessment so fill it out as best you can. You'll want to list any allergies, medical conditions, and possible concerns teachers and co-workers may need to know. The only way you could possibly mess up this form is if you lie about an illness or problem you're facing. However, if after making it into the program you suddenly discover something about your health while abroad, don't worry. It will not count against you. When I filled this form out I didn't know I suffered from low blood sugar until I spent three months in Japan and had to take precautions to ensure I didn't faint during my students' basketball practices. If you miss something by accident and it becomes worth mentioning in the interview, that is okay. Just do what you can and always be honest. It's better to discuss possible issues, than say nothing at all.

If you are undergoing any current treatment for a physical or mental health issue, or taking medication that requires a prescription and refills, or if you're frequently visiting the doctor in order to overcome surgery, you will need to submit a Statement of Physician form. The Statement of Physician form is different from the Self-Assessment Medical form, and it will require a doctor's exam and a signature. So, plan ahead and schedule the appropriate appointment if necessary. If you need to fill this out, do not be alarmed. This is not going to disqualify you. If anything, this will further help with your placement because if you need access to specific medication or physicians, the JET program will try to place you close to a hospital so you can get the help you need. Don't be afraid to include the form if you're currently undergoing any kind of treatment.

HEADS UP: If you're an early placement candidate, you will need to provide a health certificate sooner than most applicants, so keep that in mind when you're applying. This is an actual physical / medical exam that your physician will need to submit. See your application for more details.

University transcripts

These must be official university transcripts sent directly from your college and university. If you're wondering about the required GPA to be accepted into the program, there really isn't one. 3.0 is a good benchmark since it shows you're a decent student, but other than your GPA, the program wants to make sure you have an education and that you're not a psychopath or criminal.

The JET Program's online application will have specific advice and guidelines regarding credits from online schools, study abroad courses, and transcripts. The rules might change depending on your country, so be sure to check with the JET program managers and the official application to ensure you follow their guidelines. Read their instructions and follow them, and you should be just fine. *If you've graduated from multiple universities, you may need to provide a transcript from each one as proof* so it supports your information on the general application.

Degree / Proof of expected graduation

If you've already graduated, contact your school's registrar office and ask them for a copy of your diploma or degree. If you're a current student, you will need an official letter signed by an administrator stating when you expect to graduate including the month and the year. Ask for a few copies in the event you lose one between when you receive the proof of graduation and when you submit them for your application. You might also need to provide an additional copy even after making it past the interview stage. People make mistakes and sometimes the office will lose your forms like they did mine. Make sure to attach them to your application and follow the instructions to the letter.

To any undergraduates and graduates who consider applying to the JET Program, make sure you have settled all "incompletes" on your transcript. While having an incomplete in your original application will likely not eliminate you from the program, you will need to be close to settling it by the time your second interview arrives. If you don't settle the incomplete and you are unable to graduate, you will be prevented from joining the JET Program. When I was in graduate school, a handful of my classmates were at risk of not being allowed to join the JET Program as CIRs since they didn't pass their thesis examinations in the spring. They had to make arrangements with their professors to be allowed to temporarily graduate, but they had to finish their thesis while working abroad. As a result, they were unable to walk and receive their official degree until they finished. They joined the JET Program as CIRs, but they had to travel back to the U.S. for a few days the following year while working in order to graduate and fully receive their Masters degree.

Two-page statement of purpose

This is the most important piece of your application. What is difficult about this essay is the amount of content you are expected to cover within two pages. The application has specific guidelines with margins and format, so even before you start writing, format your page so it's just right. This is also a part of the test to see if you can follow instructions. For the essay you will receive a prompt with two to three questions. Some of the questions in the prompt possibly include and are not limited to:

- Why do you want to go to Japan as a JET?
- Why are you applying to be an ALT, CIR, or SEA?
- What effect do you hope to have on the local community and the international community?
- What relevant experiences or personal skills do you have and how will they contribute towards your time in the JET Program?
- What do you hope to gain professionally and personally from the JET Program?
- How will being chosen impact your future goals and career?
- How has Japan been a part of your life?
- What made you want to become a JET?

If you want to get a head start on the essay, ask yourself these questions and think about how you can answer them in a clear and concise manner that shows your professionalism, but also your thirst for adventure and ability to try new things. Just be sure to adjust your content based on what the application asks for.

Two letters of reference

This is not your typical letter where a teacher can just throw together a quick document saying how wonderful you are as a person and why you'd be a great fit for the JET program. In fact, the JET program has a specific set of rules and procedures for those writing your letter of recommendation. Be sure to print those guidelines out as soon as the application has been launched and give them plenty of time. As a good rule of thumb my professors taught me in undergrad and graduate school, three weeks is usually expected as common courtesy. After all, you're not the only person the professor has to worry about. The last thing you want is to soil a good relationship you once had with your professor because you failed to provide them the correct documents and enough time.

Also, be sure to choose references you know you can trust and who won't blackball you. Some aspiring JETs who were cut in the first round learned from the inside that their reference blackballed them in the application. Politics happen at the university level all the time, so make sure you play the game and choose wisely. The JET Program requires all recommenders to submit their letters through a special online application portal, so while you will not be able to check what a specific recommender has written, you can verify whether or not they have submitted the application on time.

Proof of citizenship

For proof of citizenship you will need to provide a copy of your passport, birth certificate or naturalization papers. Uploading a student I.D. and / or Driver's License is unacceptable. Please note as of this date of publication: *If you have dual citizenship in Japan and the U.S. you will have to forfeit your Japanese citizenship in order to apply to the JET Program.* If you currently reside in Japan and only have a temporary visitor status you will need to return to your home country and fulfill all of the application requirements for the interview in order to apply.

Second round in the application

If you've done everything right and the JET program coordinators in your area like your essay, and you fulfill all of their tasks, you will proceed to the second round. Typically, you'll hear the results of the first round of applications after Christmas. The interview will most likely take place at your local consulate where you will be given a brief 10-20-minute interview slot. Be sure to arrive early, have a seat, and relax. Due to a Non-Disclosure Agreement I signed the day of the interview, I cannot describe what exactly transpired during my interview or how I answered the questions. But I can provide some advice on how you can best prepare for your interview and how I set myself for success. Keep in mind that everyone's interview is different and mine was really different from what my friends in the JET

Program experienced. My goal here is to give you advice so you can walk in the interview with confidence, have fun, relax, and walk out of the room smiling with no regrets.

For starters, revisit your Statement of Purpose and memorize it. That doesn't mean memorize the whole essay word for word, but rather understand it and be able to recall what you wrote. This essay is your story and a display of your character when you walk into the interview. Aside from the letters of recommendation, the general application, and accomplishments, the interviewers likely determine who progresses by their essay. Your local JET coordinators saw something inside your essay they were curious about and want to follow up on. Another way to think about this step in the process is like dating.

You're not going to dive into gritty details on the first date (Statement of Purpose). The first date is when you provide a general idea of who you are and how you respond to questions. If all goes well, the person of your dreams likes you, and there is interest in a second date (the oral interview in this metaphor) to probe further. The interview is the best chance to expand further on what you wrote and answer questions that will likely come up after reading your essay.

Another way to prepare for the interview is to ask a friend or even your recommender to look at your essay and provide some questions for you to answer in a mock interview. Mock interviews are great since you can work on posture, eye contact, and answering questions not too long, and not too short. The JET Program interview was one of the best interviews I ever had in my life and it felt more like a conversation. Stick to your character and know yourself. You don't have to worry about not being good enough or being fake. You already are a likely candidate by making it this far. So, I want you to walk into that interview with a smile and just be yourself. If it makes you feel any better, I was a little nervous when I shook hands with the interviewers. I mispronounced the name of a man who introduced himself to me and I called him Mr. Hassle. Talk about an awkward first impression. Just take a deep breath before you walk in and remember to smile. Enjoy the journey.

Post interview

After your interview will come the most frustrating part of the application process: waiting for the verdict. Usually the JET Program notifies people of their interview results by mid-March or early April. There are three categories of results. 1) Short-listed. 2) Alternates. 3) Unsuccessful. If you're short-listed, congratulations! If you're an alternate, don't fret and you should still prepare to go. Lots of short-listed people back out of the JET Program in the last minute due to irresistible job opportunities, family affairs, or just a change of heart. You still have a chance of being moved up to a full-time JET anywhere between May through December in the same year.

Handling rejection

If you're rejected, do not take it personally. For whatever reason, the interviewers did not see you as a fit for the program during this time. They are not allowed to tell you why you were unsuccessful. If I were you, I'd revisit your essay and reflect on the interview and think about what wasn't represented and what the interviewers were possibly looking for. Ask yourself what you could've done better and apply it to next year's application. Just because you didn't make it in the second round, doesn't mean it's over. If you really want to be a JET and I think you do if you're still reading this, keep on trying. You can still apply for next year. Do not give up! A classmate of mine got rejected twice before making it into the program. In the end, she said the wait was worth it.

Placements

In your general application, you will have the opportunity to list three locations where you would like to be placed. While the JET Program can't make any promises, they will do their best to place you in those spots provided you give good reasons. I will speak honestly. Although I was blessed to be placed in the heart of Tokyo, most JETs will be placed in the countryside, on a tiny island, or in areas less traveled by tourists. The reason why I was placed in the city was due to the Japanese Prime Minister's political goal of placing an English teacher in every elementary, middle, and high school in Japan by the 2020 Olympics. As a result of this political agenda, the JET program expanded their program into the major cities, so I was one of 200 incoming JETs placed in Tokyo in the year 2015. I also had an advantage since I had already lived in Tokyo for a year prior to applying and mentioned it in my application. The program wanted me to be happy and knew I'd adjust immediately to life in Tokyo.

It will feel like an eternity while you wait to hear about your placements and you'll be waiting until July. You may not hear about your placement until two to three weeks before your departure. If this is the case, do not panic. Simply contact the organizer of the JET Program in your area and see if they can investigate for you. The reality is the people who decide placements are based in Tokyo, and it is a small group of people who are working around the clock calling all schools, verifying the kind of person they want, and then matching that JET with the school's request. It is going to take time, so please be patient.

HEADS UP: If you accept your position in the JET Program before you receive your placement, you shouldn't, and dare I say…MUST NOT back out of the program. There are instances where JETs suddenly quit the program due to not being placed where they wanted. No matter where you are placed you will have plenty of opportunities to travel to your ideal city. You only have to work 16 days a month, and this doesn't include the days off from school. Trust me, there will be plenty of time to travel.

If you leave the JET program before you even make it to your destination, you're doing three terrible things. I'm not saying this to guilt-trip you, but I'm saying it because it is the truth and you will make everyone's jobs much more difficult. First, you're hurting the city or school that is supposed to receive you because now they're out of a JET or CIR for an entire year. Yes, there are alternate JETs waiting in the wings, but you already had the opportunity to get out of the process a few weeks or a month ago. Since they already expected you to commit, they now have to go through the process of finding a new JET from the list of alternatives, file paper work, file a visa and get everything sorted. It's more work for them and you're going to have some issues in the future should you apply again.

Next, you're damaging your school's reputation. The coordinators of the JET program will keep your records on file so if you throw your placement school under the bus, expect similar treatment to your educational institution. It will become difficult for future aspiring JETs from your school to apply to the program and it will hurt the reputation of the recommenders who put their faith in you to succeed.

Finally, you're ruining any future chances you will have with the program. If you try to reapply after bailing due to what you thought was a poor placement, good luck applying. I doubt they'll even read your essay for round one. Sorry to be harsh, but that is the truth and after my experience in Japan, I don't want any school or city to suffer without a JET or CIR. We really do make a difference in our school and community.

Visas

This is a section you're probably not going to like and will find it tedious, but it is important. Before even applying for the Visa, you need to renew your passport. I don't care if you still have two years left on it before it expires and you're only planning to go to Japan for one year. Things happen, your life could change and you may want to stay longer. You don't want to get stranded in one country or be forced to leave Japan since you didn't consider all of the options.

First, check your passport right now and if you only have two years before it expires, renew it after you have passed your interview. The reason why is because after the interview you're going to have a few months before the JET program announces their selection. The typical visa required for the JET program is three years with a requirement to renew it while you're in Japan if you stay for a 4th year in the program. Three years is the minimum a school is required to keep you on for, and if you do a phenomenal job, you can stay for up to five years. Now let's do some math, say your passport is only valid for another two years and you have a Japanese visa for three. If your passport expires while you're in Japan, you're in hot water should you need to reapply for a visa or leave the country. Remember to renew your passport after the interview is finished for the JET application. You might need it for the interview to prove you're a U.S. citizen, so be sure to wait and renew at the appropriate time.

Packing

Hopefully by now you have received your placement and you're excited for the adventures ahead. You might be wondering, "What should I bring with me?" Although I've been to Japan more than seven times and have lived there for more than three years, I always end up bringing more than I need and I suffer for it in the long run. A general rule and outcome you should remember when packing is, you're always going to end up bringing more back with you. Whether you are coming back for a quick visit during the Christmas holidays or just finishing the program, your suitcase WILL BE OVERFLOWING.

Before I list the major do's let me say the don'ts.

Do Not Bring

1) A surfboard
2) A gigantic gaming computer / desktop computer
3) Your pet dog or cat
4) Your Aunt Margret or family member to live with you (unless they have a job lined up and you mentioned they were accompanying you in your application)
5) Your car by sea barge
6) Your bicycle (Japan has strict rules about bicycles)
7) Furniture
8) Coffee press or Keurig
9) Rice cookers
10) Hair dryers (Japan uses a different voltage and mainly two-prong outlets)
11) Cooking utensils or pots and pans
12) Laundry detergent
13) Pillows or sheets
14) Futon
15) A large musical instrument or any kind of musical instrument that requires special cases for transportation. (You can always rent or borrow while abroad)
16) An airsoft gun or paintball gun
17) Fireworks
18) Weapons
19) Drugs (That's kind of a no-brainer)
20) Skis / Snowboards
21) Japanese textbooks or dictionaries. Japan has the best books to study Japanese from that you won't find in your home area. Save yourself

the trouble and wait until you arrive before buying any language texts.

22) Your girlfriend / boyfriend / significant other *for at least the first month or two*. The reason why is because all JETs are partnered with a homestay for a few days and since Japanese homes are quite small, having an extra guest will place a burden on the homestay family. There is also a chance that if your significant other is tagging along with you, the JET program will not accommodate them and they may have to pay for everything themselves. My advice is to bring your significant other with you *AFTER you've settled and have finished the homestay and training sessions*. By that point you'll have secured your apartment, you'll be working at your new job and you can focus on helping them adjust to Japan rather than yourself.

Do Bring

1) Two suitcases
2) Camera
3) Gifts for your homestay family, supervisor, principal, and vice principal. These can be small gifts but try to get things they won't find unless they visit America. Perhaps a local candy, T-shirt, mug, silverware, stamps, collectible items, postcards, hats, etc. Use your imagination for gifts.
4) A week's worth of underwear
5) A week's worth of dress clothes to wear around the office. Men, aim for cool business attire. Ladies, aim for a mix of business outfits, but also keep sweaters and dresses. To both genders, wear nothing with low cut showing too much skin, thigh, breasts, and absolutely no short skirts. Don't wear anything with holes in them. I promise you your co-workers WILL tear you apart and criticize you for that. This isn't a Japanese cartoon, this is real life.
6) One week's worth of normal clothes. Try to pack extra for summer and for winter.
7) Sneakers and dress shoes. Two pairs of sneakers, two pairs of dress shoes.
8) A suit or something you can wear for business excursions.

9) Plenty of socks
10) Swim suit or trunks
11) Sunglasses
12) One towel
13) Mementos from home you can show the class. (Yearbook, pictures of your home, family, and hometown)
14) Little souvenirs or trinkets you could pass out to students in games.
15) A book or something to read on the plane ride. Depending on your departure area, you may be in for a 14-hour flight or longer.
16) Hand sanitizer
17) Laptop (although this could change depending on your country's travel regulations)
18) $100.00 in Japanese Yen and $100.00 - $200.00 U.S. or your country's currency.
19) Contact lens solution and cases (they're quite expensive in Japan)
20) Contact lenses and glasses
21) Energy converter
22) Dental floss
23) Deodorant
24) Tooth brush and tooth paste
25) Medicine (but keeping within Japanese regulations. Japan has made certain ingredients within drugs illegal such as Codeine. For more information on illegal pharmaceutical ingredients: check https://jp.usembassy.gov/u-s-citizen-services/local-resources-of-u-s-citizens/doctors/importing-medication/)
26) Small Items you can use for activities
27) Your positive attitude and excitement

Budget

I can't stress enough how important it is to prepare a budget before you go abroad. Everyone's budget is going to be different. You may or may not have student loans due, a dear Aunt Sally who gave you a nice fortune, or be placed in an area with expensive housing. You'll hear this a lot as you prepare for your adventure, "everyone's situation is different." What I can recommend though is to bring about $10,000.00 worth of startup money if you're placed in a large city and around $7,000.00 if you're in the countryside. As you can guess, food and housing are more expensive in the major cities. While this amount of money might seem costly, you'll have a nice cushion in case something goes wrong.

When I went abroad to Japan I had around $10,000.00 saved up and ended up using about $4,000. This included two months' worth of rent, paying student loans, food, and furniture. Although this was my own budget, I'll provide you a list of things to consider in your budget and let you adapt appropriately.

Note that the value of the yen fluctuates daily and it can go anywhere from 85 yen to 120 yen per dollar. At the time of writing this, the conversion rate was 111 yen to the dollar. To keep things simple, I always thought of it as 100 yen (one coin) = one U.S. dollar. The yen currency can be divided into coins: one-yen coin, five-yen coin, 10-yen coin, 50-yen coin, 100-yen coin, 500-yen coin. When it comes to bills, the smallest value is 1,000 yen (around $10.00) followed by 5,000 yen ($50.00), and then 10,000 yen ($100.00). My biggest piece of advice to you is to keep and use your change before using your bills. Your money will travel a long way and you won't be visiting the bank as much.

Possible Budget Items:

- Several dollars in Japanese Yen.
- Two months' worth of rent (ranging between 60,000 to 160,000 yen in total. This is so you can include your additional one month's deposit as almost all realtors require this when you rent)
- Approximately 10,000 yen for utilities during your first month
- One month's worth of grocery money
- Furnishings for the apartment: futon or bed, pillows, sheets, a desk, fridge, washing machine, lights, mini shelving unit or bookcase, chairs, a pole to hang clothes from, hangers, towels, trash bins, television, clothing drawers
- Money for train tickets
- Student loans
- Money to eat out for two weeks before you receive your first paycheck and settle your housing.
- Vacuum cleaner
- Bicycle if you'd like to purchase one from a shop

- Cooking utensils and supplies
- Cell phone (**<u>NECESSARY</u>**)
- Internet connection at your home (most likely not provided for you)
- Money for entertainment so you can explore and have fun with other JETs

Night shot of downtown Ikebukuro. This is where I lived.

Chapter 2: Yōkoso -> Welcome to Japan

First week in Japan

If you've made it, congratulations! You're officially a JET and have touched down in Japan for what is likely your first time. I'm sure you have a mix of emotions running through you, and it's okay. I'm going to walk you through your first week. On day one you're going to be met by several Japanese locals at the airport who will take your luggage and help you get situated. While you can take two suitcases with you to Japan, you will only be allowed to take one suitcase with you to the hotel since you're sharing a small hotel room with two to three other JETs. Transfer what you need right now into a smaller suitcase or better yet prepare ahead of time before you leave home for the airport. Your second suitcase will be taken to storage and be waiting for you at the school two weeks from when you arrive in Japan.

The locals will then take you to your hotel where you'll be partnered with a roommate or two for orientation and you will be free to explore the area. My recommendation on this day is to do what you feel most comfortable with. Get some food nearby with a couple JETs. Let your loved ones know that you've arrived safely in Tokyo by sending them an email at the computer lounge (though I'm guessing the line is long for that), and exchange some currency at the hotel's automated machine. No matter what be sure to rest and get ready for tomorrow morning. You'll be likely tossing and turning due to the jet lag, but you'll get over it within a week.

Days 2 - 7 will involve orientation. Dress in formal business attire since the organizational heads of the JET Program and several alumni will visit your hotel, present, and run various training seminars. Wake up early with your fellow JETs, get dressed and eat breakfast. Day two will involve a lot of speeches and opportunities to get to know other JETs and break the ice. Orientation will last anywhere from four days to a week. There will be some fun parts, and some really dull parts, but I'm here to help. Below are some common problems JETs encountered during orientation and my answers to them.

Here are some survival tips on how to make the most of your situation:

Problem: How do I exchange currency?

Solution: You can exchange currency from dollars to yen at the hotel lobby. There should be a machine in the Shinjuku Plaza Hotel (this is where the last orientation was held) and you can just insert what you want exchanged and get a great rate. Exchanging your money at the machine is actually better than doing it at the airport or at the bank in your home country.

Problem: How do I get access to Wi-Fi? All I have is my American cell phone and I'm afraid to go on it due to possibly using the international signals and roaming.

Solution: Step 1. Go into your settings and turn off Roaming and then put your phone on airplane mode. Step 2. Your American phone should still be able to sense the Wi-Fi available even in the hotel lobby. Connect to it and check your emails, Facebook, whatever you use to contact home.

Problem: I don't have a place to live yet and I just got here and was told I have a week to find a home.

Solution: For starters, the middleman company JET chose to help incoming JETs should have contacted you before arriving. If they haven't, notify one of the JET counselors of your situation and they should be able to phone the middleman company and see what the holdup is.

Once you receive an email from the middleman company, they will ask you for an ideal budget in yen for rent, and then ideal location and preferences such as a one-room apartment, proximity to train station, and age of the building. The JET program will give you a few days to meet with realtors and scout some locations to find your ideal apartment. So, relax. Everything is going to be okay. I promise you will not be starving on the street after orientation. I dive into housing later on in this guide so you can skip ahead there if you want.

Problem: I don't know anybody!

Solution: Walk up to a JET and introduce yourself. I encourage you to be awkward and outgoing at this stage in the game, and the more you put yourself out there the better. Everyone is in the same boat as you and while they might put up a cool façade, deep down they will feel relieved that someone reached out to them and started a conversation. While not all of the JETs you meet at orientation will be in the same city or be teaching the same grade level, having contacts across Japan can be helpful when you want a travel companion or tour a certain location. You should NETWORK, NETWORK, NETWORK. Also, pay attention to announcements and get on Facebook or whatever social media group is active for people in your area. Before I arrived, I joined my JET's Tokyo Facebook group and they were already planning events and dinner parties after orientation. If you don't see anyone starting something, be the instigator and get something going. Ask some people you just met if they want to grab lunch or dinner. Be sure to tag along if someone announces they're getting ramen or some kind of Japanese food.

Problem: I want to go out and drink, but am not sure if it's okay for orientation.

Solution: DO NOT GET SMASHED DURING THIS WEEK! You're going to be meeting people from all over the world and meeting local leaders from the Board of Education, the JET Program, and possibly some political figures. The last thing you want is to look and smell like a hot mess the following morning after your night on the town. Enjoy the local cuisine and have a beer if you want, but don't get smashed. Know your limits. Stick to your itinerary and represent your country. There will be plenty of time to test the local brews after you've settled into your apartment and have gotten used to your job.

Problem: I feel sick.

Solution: There is a med kit for JETs at the hotel and you can ask someone nearby where it is. If you need help with medicine, you can also ask hotel staff who are bilingual or even a friend for help. If you brought your own meds you should be okay. Excuse yourself when necessary and do what you have to do.

HEADS UP: Keep a bottle of hand sanitizer on you and wash your hands before eating. You are meeting hundreds of people really quickly and you're going to be cramped in small spaces for long periods of time, so germs will spread. People will get sick. That is a promise. Having that hand sanitizer could make a difference in you enjoying orientation, or keeling over wishing you could crawl back to bed. Plan ahead!

Problem: I already know everything they're teaching and I'm bored as hell and I think this is ridiculous.

Solution: Well I won't lie. You are right in that some of these teaching methods from lesson planning to how to calm students are just not going to work. Most of the lesson plans people suggest to you are from those who don't even teach anymore. Let's face it, someone at their office probably told them to come up with a mock lesson of what a JET could possibly teach and present at the conference. So, do you have a right to be bored? Absolutely! Does this give you the right to be a jerk and not participate? No!

Here's how you can make the activities more engaging and thus cause time to pass by. Actively engage in the events by asking questions, and take notes on what you would want to change if you were forced to implement the speakers' ideas. If you're asked to come up with a mock lesson plan, try to create entertaining examples and see how people react. The point I'm making is while you do have to participate, you can make the most of a dull situation by using your sense of humor and positive attitude.

Week two of orientation: Housing
If you skipped ahead to this section, I don't blame you. Most JETs worry about their housing as soon as they arrive. After all it is your home for the next year or possibly longer, and you want it to be good.

Apartment or share house?
Before you arrive in Japan you should ask yourself whether or not you want to live in an apartment or a share house, a much larger house with a kitchen and several bathrooms shared by many people. Each has its own advantages and disadvantages and will depend on your budget. Share houses can be really cheap if you live in the country and expensive depending on the location in Tokyo. Some can range from $300.00 to $900.00 a month depending on location and space inside. If you live in a share house you're going to have to share utensils, cooking ware, bathrooms and shower space

with people. Some of the responsibilities will be handled for you, but some you must handle yourself. Meanwhile living inside an apartment can provide you with peace, but you'll be left to your own devices and it'll fall solely on you to maintain the cleanliness and structure of the apartment while staying on top of rent and utility payments.

How to rent an apartment

The JET program will provide you with a contract company or middleman who will guide you through the process of renting an apartment. The advantage of using this middleman company is that it serves as your guarantor. When renting an apartment in Japan, you need a guarantor, usually a Japanese citizen or someone with residency. Since most foreign visitors to Japan do not know anyone, it can be difficult to get an actual apartment other than a share house if you don't have the right connections. Thankfully, the middleman company takes care of that issue. On top of that, almost all of the apartments within the middleman company's database will be foreigner-friendly.

As I mentioned earlier, during the summer before you arrive you should have received an email from your assigned realtor or middleman. They will ask you for a budget, ideal location, distance from the train, preferred room size, etc. They will then provide you with a list of 10-20 properties for you to look at and you should decide on three to four before meeting them face-to-face. The apartment choices will most likely be in Japanese and English. If need be, you can still decide on possible choices at your personal meeting with them, so don't feel upset if you don't have time to look at your choices during orientation.

When you meet the middleman company for two to three days, you're going to be sitting down with them in a room with a couple of other JETs looking for housing. Once you all decide on target locations to visit, the middlemen will drive you to two or three locations per person. It will be you and several other JETs cramped in a vehicle, so be prepared to sit all day and look at apartments in the hot sun. Bring sunscreen, water, and stay hydrated. One of the representatives of the apartment should be present, so you should ask them various questions. Keep in mind none of the utilities work, so it won't be possible to try everything just yet. Although I liked my apartment, you might want to ensure the apartment is what you're looking for by asking:

1. Is there already an Internet connection or can I get my own Wi-Fi in the apartment? How fast is it?
2. Does the heating and air conditioning work? If not, who do I call? (I was without air conditioning for the first two weeks in my place during the hot summer)
3. How do I turn on the gas?
4. Are space heaters allowed?
5. Are there any particular rules in this neighborhood? (Such as where to place trash, noise levels at night)
6. Are roaches a problem here? (Turns out the apartment building next door to me was evicted and sealed off due to a roach problem)
7. Where is the nearest grocery store?
8. Is there a key money payment? (Read the HEADS UP below)

Once you decide on a location, you will return to the office the next day with your fellow JETs to contact the owners of the properties. They may interview you over the phone depending on how comfortable they are with foreigners. Don't be alarmed or offended. Just do your best to answer all of the questions.

After selecting an apartment and passing the screening, you will be given a housing contract to sign. Usually these contracts last two years, so be sure to check the fine print to see if there is a penalty for breaking contract early. In addition to signing you will likely have to put a down payment on the apartment to help pay for cleaning when you move out or any damages. You will receive some of that down payment back when you move out provided there are no problems. This amount usually costs one month's worth of rent, so if you feel like you paid two months' worth of rent at first, do not be alarmed. This is normal.

HEADS UP: There is another form of payment you may come across, but I've noticed this is becoming increasingly rare. On some occasions when you rent an apartment, there is a special fee called "key money" or *rei kin* 礼金 in Japanese. This is where the owner of the apartment expects the renter to pay up to a month or even a year's worth of rent up front as a thank you gift for allowing them to stay in the apartment. This is an old tradition that is thankfully, gradually dying out. To avoid some awkward financial tension, it is worth asking if there is a key money fee expected in the price. It should state this in English on your forms, but be sure to ask just to be safe.

If you jump through all of the hoops and hurdles in this process, you'll be given a visiting date for the apartment where you and the realtor and the middleman will go inspect the apartment once more and go over any concerns you might have. During this time, they will show you where you have to dump the garbage, where you can find the owner, how to contact the gas, water and electric companies should you run into any problems, and where to evacuate in the event of a natural disaster. Each realtor has their own rules when it comes to the number of keys provided and penalties involved if you lose keys, so be sure to pay attention and keep your documents organized and filed away. If you see any documents in the cabinet below the stove or in a particular area that discusses details of the gas, electricity or water in your apartment, do not write on them and do not throw them away. You will need to save these documents for the next tenant and you might be checked as to whether or not you kept them in good condition when you leave.

Why is it difficult to get housing in Japan as a foreigner?

Believe it or not, there have been multiple cases where exchange students and tourists have been refused entry to hotels, apartments, bars and even restaurants. It can be easy to blame this problem on racism, but it's much more complicated than that. Put yourself in their position. You've lived on an island-nation for most of your life surrounded by people of your own skin tones or color and who speak the same language as you. One day at your job at a hotel, a stranger who doesn't look like anything you've seen before and does not speak your language wants entry and possibly permission to lodge. Other than the fact you might feel uncomfortable, there's the issue of communication. If there was a fire drill or if something happened and you needed to communicate with that person, and for whatever reason they were harmed, you could be blamed for it. So, to avoid this communication issue and liability, a few Japanese people will turn away foreign customers. It's not personal, it's just the idea of autonomy and having a smooth business. This same ideology applies to realtors. There are some who are reluctant to rent to foreigners, and it just happened that the apartment I wanted, was owned by one of these people who was suspicious of foreigners.

I remember the experience quite well because I was grilled twice by the owners of the apartment. First the middleman company told me it was unlikely I would get the apartment since they didn't think I could speak Japanese. As soon as they said that, I immediately began to speak and proved to them I could negotiate over the phone. Some of you who read this may think I'm generalizing, but I'm telling you my story. The middlemen called up the representative of the owners and we talked over the phone. He asked me a series of questions such as what time I usually go to bed, was I planning to have raucous parties, would I be willing to only communicate in Japanese? etc. It was a long list and our conversation lasted a good 20 minutes over the phone. In the end, I got the apartment, but this proves that it isn't racism that gets in the way of people wanting an apartment, but rather can the person provide the same likelihood of autonomy and success the Japanese owner is used to.

If you go with a private rental company, you will likely face an uphill battle. You will be responsible for researching a guarantor, getting the guarantor to sign on your behalf, researching properties and negotiating with people who may or may not accept foreign residents. Many realtors and owners in Japan don't feel comfortable renting to foreigners due to previous incidents of neglecting to pay rent and suddenly leaving the country, damaging the apartments, loud parties, and fear of not being able to speak the language and communicate. Clearing up the reputation of foreigners will be one of the most frustrating challenges you will face while working abroad.

Although there may be better offers on apartments out there if you speak the language and can jump through all of the obstacles, the JET program's realtor assignments are the easiest way to proceed. It also lowers the risk of you not having an apartment and living in a hotel or karaoke room for an extra week, which can be quite expensive.

Your homestay

After you've survived the first week of orientation and selected an apartment, you'll likely be placed with a homestay family for a few days. Staying with a homestay family is a rare opportunity to see what life is like for Japanese locals, and exchange your cultures. I'm going to give you some advice so you don't offend your host family or make a fool of yourself.

As soon as you see your host family, give them a bow and shake their hand at the same time. This way they feel a little more comfortable since you're mixing their bowing culture with the Western tradition of shaking hands. If you want to only bow in Japanese, that's fine too, but to only give a handshake might weird-out some people. Next, you'll want to introduce yourself in Japanese.

Say: *Hajimemashite. Watashi wa* (your name) *desu. Kyō kara dōzo yoroshiku onegaishimasu.* 初めまして。私は（　　）です。今日からどうぞよろしくお願いします。

Meaning: How do you do. My name is…… Nice to meet you today.

Note: *Yoroshiku onegaishimasu* has loads of different translations, but we'll stick with this for now.

Hopefully the JET program partnered you with a family that knows some English if you have no Japanese background. Thank them in advance for allowing you to stay in their home and then let the conversation flow. If you experience awkward silence, talk about the weather. This is a common way for Japanese people to break the ice when they meet someone for the first time. It allows them to set a common area of agreement. I used to think Japanese people were weird when they kept saying almost every day for the first few months, *"Kyō wa ii tenki desu ne."* 今日はいい天気ですね。 "The weather sure is nice today isn't it." I wanted to say "Well duh. That's obvious." but that was just their way of trying to reach out to me and start a conversation without being too intrusive.

Entering the house

First things first before you even enter the house. Bow before the doorway and say *"osewa ni narimasu."* お世話になります。 It literally means "I'm in your care." This may seem strange and your host family might say, "You are more Japanese than me or you're very Japanese." That is okay. The family will know you are doing your best to respect their culture and traditions despite the lack of cultural knowledge or language skills. The effort will go a long way in building a good impression. *Osewa ni narimasu* is an expression that shows you're putting yourself in someone else's care and that you respect them. The Japanese have a long history with respecting homes, land, and even objects that have been passed down for generations. If you'd like to read more about this connection and respect for objects and spiritual beliefs, you can read my master's thesis page at http://scholarworks.umass.edu/cgi/viewcontent.cgi?article=1276&context=m asters_theses_2

Next step, take off your shoes and BE SURE TO WEAR CLEAN SOCKS! If you aren't wearing clean socks, change into some before entering the house. While this is not necessarily a deal-breaker, it's almost like a symbol that you might look good on the outside, but deep down you're just a smelly person who doesn't know the meaning of hygiene and self-respect. Make sure you pack clean socks for when you meet your host family. Barefoot is okay as well.

Let the family show you around the house and explain some rules about your living quarters. Make sure you follow these rules exactly and you'll be okay. With regards to presenting your gifts, I'd suggest waiting until after dinner once the family has settled down into the living room area. This way you can enjoy some quality time with your host family before bed.

HEADS UP: If given a social outing choice, always spend time with your host family as long as you remain in their care. While they might say you're welcome to hang out with friends and do your own thing, you really should do your best to spend time with your host family. Think about it, this family has taken time out of their busy schedules to host you and get you acclimated to the culture. To ignore that opportunity is not only a waste of a golden moment, but also kind of a slap in the face to their hospitality.

When I was staying with my host family, I had to rush over to one of my Japanese friend's homes who was also my former host mother when I was a student in Tokyo. She was in great pain and her life was possibly at risk. Weighing the options between my host family and saving one of my friends I obviously chose my friend whom I was previously indebted to. I couldn't tell the host family exactly what I was doing, so I told them one of my JET friends needed some help and that I wouldn't make it to dinner. I gave them several hours' notice and they said it was fine. I helped my friend and made a difference in my former host family's life, but the next day I couldn't help but notice my current host family treated me differently. Sure, we chatted as usual, but it wasn't the same as the previous nights.

After my time was over, the family never returned my emails or offers to hang out. Granted they were in their 70s, so that may have had an effect, but I couldn't help but feel I was at fault. This outcome was unfortunate because I was forced to choose between saving a life and spending time with my host family. The message here folks is: *the Japanese can be difficult to win back if you have offended them in any way.* So be sure to weigh your options carefully. I would've made the same decision despite knowing the outcome, but be aware that your excuse to not spend time with your host family better be a really good one. If all goes well, your host family will keep in contact with you during your period as a JET and you guys can hang out and explore the city, or if you're lucky, maybe even go on vacations together as some of my JET friends have.

Day one in your new apartment

If you've gotten this far in your adventure, congratulations! Now we got to click on survival mode. By the end of your five days with the homestay family, you'll be given permission to move into the apartment. Now you might think you'll be able to relax, except a couple of problems remain. You will likely have no bed, no lights, and no furniture. Yikes! On day one of moving into your new apartment, focus on the following:

- getting a futon or at least some blankets to sleep on to make a bed until your real bed arrives
- going to the ward office to register your address
- purchasing a lamp,
- getting some basic cooking tools for your first meal. If you want to eat outside and have the money to do so, that's fine, but focus on getting your apartment set up.

Registering at the ward office

Once you arrive inside your apartment, one of the first things you have to do is register your address at the local ward office known as a *kuyakusho* 区役所. This is an absolute must because the Japanese government needs to keep tabs on you to make sure you're not trying to immigrate illegally into their country. Failure to register your address can lead to hefty financial penalties. In my opinion, it's best to take care of this sooner rather than later before you're busy with your new job.

If possible, go early on a weekday to the ward office. Usually you have within the first two weeks of moving into the apartment to register, so you can have your supervisor arrange your schedule so you can make it. Once you enter the ward office someone will help direct you to the appropriate station where you'll fill out some forms and then be required to wait for 40 minutes to an hour, so I recommend bringing a book. If you go to the ward office past 2:00pm and you live in the city, I guarantee you will be there for a good three or possibly four hours waiting. Believe me that is not fun and I made that mistake when I first moved to Tokyo.

Health insurance

All JETs have four kinds of insurance during their time in the program: National Health Insurance, Pension Insurance, Employment Insurance, and Accident insurance. The ward office is responsible for securing your National Health Insurance and they will do so by giving you a temporary I.D. Keep this I.D. card with you at all times. If you want to get reduced rates when you have to go to the hospital, you will need your card on you. Keep in my mind though that this is a temporary card and it will no longer work once the ward office mails you the official national health insurance card. Once you receive this card, keep it in your wallet. For more information on the various forms of health insurance and how they affect you on the program, visit http://jetprogramme.org/en/insurance/

Foreigner Card

The last item and probably the most important the ward office will give you is your foreign resident card known as *zairyū kādo* 在留カード in Japanese. It will have your name, visitor status (educator, student, businessman, entertainer etc.) and the length of time you're allowed to reside in Japan as stated on your passport. Whatever you do, **do not lose this card and keep it on your person (preferably in your wallet) at all times**. The reason why is because it is likely that at some point, police officers will pull you over and ask to see your residence card. You cannot ignore this request. You have to show it to them and if you don't have it on you, you could face a $100.00 fine and several hours of interrogation at one of their offices. On top of that, the officers will have the right to follow you home to verify your address and prove that you live in that location and then they will photograph your room with you in it. This is not illegal. This is unfortunately standard operating procedure, and I pray you never have to face this kind of treatment while you're living in Japan. It is not a fun process, but it is a necessary act for the police to keep tabs on all visitors and to ensure the safety of the populace. Now you can start to see why Japan has one of the lowest crime rates. If you misplace your foreigner card, be sure to notify the police immediately and fill out the information at a *kōban* or local police box. They may give you a document showing you've lost it and you can have something to show police should you get stopped. Japan has a great system when it comes to lost items, so hopefully it will turn up. If a week or two goes by and nothing happens, you'll likely have to get it replaced at the ward office, but it shouldn't cost you anything.

Note: Your standard residence card. If your zairyū kādo has a hole in it, that means it is marked as invalid.

Rent or buy furniture?

If you've followed my instructions, hopefully you'll have settled your insurance and registration at the ward office on day one. Now it's time for the fun part: furnishing your apartment. When moving into your apartment, there likely won't be much. If you don't have much time to take care of major shopping, at the very least buy a pillow, a blanket and a lamp. This way you can have a little light in your apartment, because most likely the built-in lighting won't be enough to illuminate the area. You'll also have enough materials to sleep on the floor and then on your second day, you can get what you need to really settle in.

Before you've even purchased these basic items, you'll have gotten an idea of whether you should buy or rent the remaining household items. If you're staying for more than two years and hope to immigrate and start a new life in Japan, buying furniture is a good idea and then you can sell it down the road or keep it. There are several places to buy furniture such as recycling shops, BICamera, IKEA, and others.

On the other hand, if you only want to see Japan for one year, renting furniture might be your easiest bet. It beats the hassle of throwing things away and often times the renting company will come pick up your furniture at the very end. Of course, any furniture you damage in the process will have to be paid for, but if you're careful, everything should work out. https://www.leasejapan.com/ and https://www.cortglobal.com/japan/ are good places to start looking for ideas on furniture prices. You can type in your city name and find the nearest rental store partner available when you're ready to discuss the details.

Whether you decide to rent or buy, here is a list of items you'll likely need:
- Washing machine
- Bed (read my section on insects)
- Blankets
- Refrigerator
- Slippers
- Pots and pans and skillet
- Chairs
- Desk
- Bookshelves
- Shower mat
- Towels
- Plastic cabinets for clothes
- Laundry hamper
- Drinking glasses
- Vacuum cleaner

- Broom and dustpan
- Rice cooker
- Glass jars
- Forks, knives, spoons
- Mini oven
- Toaster

HEADS UP: For large furniture such as a bed, laundry machine or refrigerator, you will have to schedule a delivery and be present when they arrive. The movers can also connect and set up your bed, refrigerator, and laundry machine for a small additional fee of around $30.00. Make sure you tell them at the store though that you want assistance connecting everything, otherwise you might struggle for hours trying to figure out how to connect the washing machine to your waterline. If you don't tell them they won't do it, so be sure to say so at the store when you schedule the delivery dates.

How to open a bank account

This section can become one of the most frustrating parts about being a JET: negotiating and attempting to open a bank account in Japan. You may think you don't need it, but you do because you otherwise won't be able to access your funds easily. For example, if you were to deposit the paychecks from your school to an American account, the money will be transferred to dollars and then back to yen when you withdraw from an ATM in Japan. I used to do this in the beginning and trust me, losing money due to currency conversion rates is not fun. Also, the schools cannot wire money into an American bank account, so a Japanese account is absolutely necessary.

Now you have a few options when it comes to banks. You have Shinsei bank, Mizuho, Mitsui and others. Your JET counselors and coordinators will go over some of the various bank options and provide some recommendations for you during your orientation session. Depending on the year, a bank may have a special offer specifically for those working in the JET Program, so you should have some good choices. Once you decide on the bank for you, it's time to visit the different bank branches. Here's the problem you will undoubtedly face and the Japanese are still strict about this today. In order to open a Japanese bank account, you have to have a

Japanese cell phone and the other issue is you have to have a Japanese bank account in order to purchase a Japanese cell phone. Talk about a real catch-22. So how do you get around it?

When you're filling out the paper work and the office worker at the bank asks for your Japanese cell phone number, put down your supervisor's number. I had my supervisor act as a bridge by getting permission to use their personal cell phone number. Then once my account was established with online banking, I changed the information online. Whatever you do, do not tell them this is your supervisor's number. If you fail for whatever reason, walk to a different branch office and try again.

HEADS UP: When you establish your account, you will be given a cash card. This is not a credit card. Think of it as a simple ATM card that will allow you to make deposits and withdrawals. If you want a credit card, you'll be able to apply for one at your bank after you've been a resident in Japan for more than six months and have been a member of a particular bank. You may also be given the option to obtain a Visa credit card when you sign up for a cell phone plan or Internet plan. These cards can be useful, but be careful of any monthly charges or special payments you need to make.

In addition to the cash card, eventually your bank will send you a special power card with numbers and letters on the back in columns. Keep this card and don't lose it! This is used for logging into online banking so you can pay rent to whatever housing agency you're using.

How to pay your student loans

If you have student loans you can pay them by placing a call to your bank to transfer the money internationally and then pay from your U.S. account. Depending on your loan provider they may or may not accept payments directly from foreign banks, which is why you may have to transfer any funds you have to a U.S. bank first and then pay. This is possible to accomplish since nowadays most Japanese banks have English-speaking staff who can help you on weekdays. They're pretty good and not once did they mess up my payments. This may have changed since I was abroad, but there are no automatic payments, so anytime you want to pay a student loan, you have to call your bank in Japan each month.

As much as I love Japan, there is one system that you may have frustration with and that is banks and ATM machines. The problem is banks operate on a 9 to 5 schedule and they have no separate ATM machine rooms. At least this was the case when I was in Tokyo. Since the banks would close at 5:00 pm, this also meant so did the ATM machines. Which meant that depending on your bank you may have to pay a service charge if you want to withdraw money from an ATM machine at a convenience store, which is open 24 hours. All post offices have an ATM machine that will accept US cards as long as they have a chip in them, but they too close at 5:00 pm and sometimes earlier. Keep this in mind when you're choosing your bank.

If you are unable to use your U.S. debit card or credit card at an ATM machine, you can try putting it upside down and switching the direction you insert the card. If that doesn't work, go to the post office since they will have the type of machine that will accept almost all U.S. and other foreign bank cards. While my U.S. cards wouldn't work at Seven Eleven stores, they always worked at post office ATMs in case I needed some emergency funds from home.

How to set up Internet

Internet can be tricky, but I've heard services are improving. If you're in the city, you will likely have very fast Internet, and I even found the Internet to be faster than what I had in the U.S.A. You're going to be dealing with one or two companies in this process. NTT Japan is the Internet service provider who will attach a fiber optic cable to your home and can get you LAN Internet and also Wi-Fi. If you'd like, you can also get a reduced fee by bundling your Internet with your phone bill and get a faster connection if you get an extension through your cellphone company. This allowed me to get much faster Internet since I noticed my connection was slowing down with only the NTT Japan connection. By bundling you also get reduced phone bills so this can be a plus.

Personally, I purchased my Internet and phone at Y-mobile and used Softbank. Once I had an account, I could go to any branch store in Tokyo and get assistance regarding my Internet and phone. When I was attempting to establish an account, the clerk walked me through all of the steps and explained what would happen based on the plan I choose.

Now I don't want you to be alarmed, but the staff at the phone company and Internet company will say that "construction" is required to set up the Wi-Fi connection. Don't let the word "construction" scare you. This is just standard talk and the so-called construction is merely setting up a wireless signal on top of some telephone lines several hundred feet away from your apartment and then checking the connection with your wireless router. No one is going to be drilling at your apartment building, so you can tell the landlord to not panic if you need to get their permission. I remember having to ask my owner's permission and when I calmly explained the situation that'd I like to Skype with my family and be able to work from home on some weekends, they understood and gave me their blessing. The key was explaining that the construction is easy to do and easy to remove. Which is true. This is not a lie.

HEADS UP: Construction shouldn't take more than 25 to 40 minutes, but the one-time fee for the construction is going to be around $300 to $400. This is added to your phone bill at a later month, so don't be surprised if you suddenly get a huge bill two months after the construction is over. It's okay! Do not panic.

Television yes or no?

Let's talk television. Everyone has their own opinion on this subject, but before I go into mine I will explain the benefits of having a television and why it could be a useful tool in your household.

Pros of having a television

Owning a television allows you to keep up to date with news in the country and abroad so you are "in the know". Due to the lack of channels compared to the U.S., everyone tends to watch the same content. If you figure which channels your colleagues and students watch late at night, you can keep up with them and participate more in daily conversations inside and outside of the office. Having a television in your home also provides 24/7 access to Japanese playing in the background which is great for those who want additional listening practice. Lastly, having a television playing in the background can be comforting if you just want to listen and pretend to have someone in the room. Living alone can be tough mentally, so having that television in the background when you're alone can help provide some comfort.

Cons of having a television

This is a small problem among many, but a majority of Japanese television shows are cooking channels with one-time celebrities nervously shaking a piece of food on their fork, biting into it and then saying "*umai*" or "*oishii*" meaning "delicious!" After hearing that for the 50th time, it gets old really quick. In addition to paying for whatever services you want or even if you just want the national television that is available to everyone, you still have to pay a service fee to NHK or the National Broadcasting Company in Japan. This is a monthly fee ranging from $13 to $20. You have to pay this fee if you own a television and there is no escaping it.

NHK is able to track down anyone who moves into an apartment or house and they will send a representative to come to your apartment and demand an instant cash payment. Even if you don't have a television, NHK will attempt to send someone to your home if someone nearby has a television, since owning a television in Japan is considered the cultural norm. There are some ways to stall the inevitable if you want to go the bad boy route of not paying for television. One way is to not answer the door at all. Another is by answering the door, giving the person a weird look and say, "*terebi wo tabemasen*" which translates to "I don't eat televisions". This implies you don't know a single word of Japanese and the clerk feels awkward because they likely don't know any English so they get scared and run off. You can also lie and say you don't have a television and pray to the Gods the NHK man doesn't attempt to barge in. But to be honest, it's just easier to pay and it is more respectful and the right thing to do since this is supposedly the only way NHK makes any money according to their website: https://www.nhk.or.jp/corporateinfo/english/receivingfee/index.html

Although owning a television has its perks, dealing with monthly payments while you're repaying student loans can be a real pain, so that is why I ended up foregoing the television and getting my news and media content via the web. Some NHK members may attempt to trick you into paying by saying you owe money if you are connected to the Internet. This is not true and can be rightfully ignored and even the police will take your side if you want to get them involved. If the NHK representative is still adamant you must pay NHK for the Internet, call up your supervisor and they will argue a way out of the situation. They want you to succeed in Japan, so they should be more than willing to help you if you feel uncomfortable.

Garbage pickup

Japan is a very clean society due to its garbage and recycling system. What you might be used to in your home country is likely very different in Japan. Each ward or region has a different recycling schedule. Typically, it is divided into burnable garbage two days a week, plastics one day, cardboards and newspapers another day, and a special day to recycle batteries, broken lightbulbs, or dangerous objects. This was my typical schedule when I lived in Ikebukuro, but it will most likely be different for you. To find out what the schedule is you can refer to the sheet given to you by your local ward office or you can go to your ward office's website. Or type into Google.com (name of your area + *gomi shūshū* ゴミ収集) garbage pickup in Japanese.

Common Terms you should know to navigate the garbage collection sites

Japanese Characters	Pronunciation	Translation
ゴミ	gomi	trash
収集	shūshū	collecting
月曜日	Getsu yōbi	Monday
火曜日	Ka yōbi	Tuesday
水曜日	Sui yōbi	Wednesday
木曜日	Moku yōbi	Thursday
金曜日	Kin yōbi	Friday
土曜日	Do yōbi	Saturday
日曜日	Nichi yōbi	Sunday

びん、カン、ペットボトル	Bin, kan, petto botoru	Glass, cans, plastic bottles
紙、布類	Kami、furui	Paper, clothing
燃やすごみ	Moyasu gomi	Burnable trash
金属	Kinzoku	metals
陶器	tōki	porcelain
ガラスごみ	Garasu gomi	Glass trash
第 1、2、3、4	Dai ichi, ni, san, yon	#1, 2, 3, 4

When disposing your garbage, you will want to either throw it out before bed or early in the morning as soon as you wake up. Personally, I'd throw out my garbage at night before bed in the event I oversleep or am just in a rush and don't have time in the morning. Unlike in the U.S. where garbage pickup is usually once a week to collect everything, if you miss the pickup, you have to wait a whole week until the designated collector for that kind of trash returns. If you attempt to mix your garbage, for example plastics with burnable, the garbage company has the right to refuse your garbage. You also can't leave your garbage out too early because typically there is no large dumpster or place to put it except out on the side of the road with everyone else's garbage.

Also of note is that neighborhoods in Japan are typically a lot more close-knit due to the close proximity to each other. If you break the rules by tossing garbage into other collection areas or if you mix your garbage with other people's waste, you might get a nasty note from a neighbor and you might even get fined if you're a repeat offender and get tracked down. As a general rule of thumb, you should dispose of your garbage as soon as possible, in the appropriate manner or else you may attract unwanted pests.

Note: This is not my garbage, but I found this note of interest since it was in my neighborhood's garbage collection spot. The message says "you're being watched as you toss your garbage in our area. Toss your garbage in your own area before you return to your home."

Roaches

Although I lived next to what was said to be an infested house that was condemned and abandoned, I only dealt with roaches a few times during my 1.8 years as a JET. Let me tell you, these Asian roaches are huge! The biggest ones I've killed were about the size of my fist. They're jet black and they move fast. Watching them crawl is like something out of a horror movie. If you want to prevent roaches, here are some precautions you can take.

Step 1: As soon as you move in, put a bait trap at the entrance or landing of your apartment.

Step 2: Purchase yourself a can of roach spray and shaving cream from your local super market. I've heard stories from other JETs where they were able to kill some of the roaches by just shooting them with shaving cream. For some reason these roaches react poorly to shaving cream, but you won't know until you try.

Step 3: Keep your bathroom, kitchen, and all of the floors clean. Don't leave out any garbage overnight if you can avoid it. I also recommend vacuuming once a week on weekends. Clean out the shower drain once every two weeks, and don't let your rooms get smelly.

Step 4: Get yourself off the floor by purchasing a bed. There are usually bed sales throughout the year, so you should be able to get yourself a good one.

Step 5: Avoid cooking smelly food, and if you do happen to cook smelly food, dispose of it immediately and air-out your apartment via screen door before the roaches visit late at night.

Step 6: Close the vents at the bottom of your front door. Supposedly this is a common entryway for them at night.

If you follow these steps you should reduce your encounters with roaches drastically, but if you do see them, don't panic. Let's hope they're more afraid of you than you are of them.

Packages
Japan's postal service runs a little differently from what you might be used to. Due to a majority of Japan's residents being out of the house and in the work force, post offices can deliver packages on weekends and even into the late hours up to 10:00 pm at night. The package will be delivered to

your door often between the early hours of the morning and afternoon. If you miss the delivery, you can have it delivered to your local convenience store and you can pick it up. Depending on the size of the package, and the delivery company, your goods may or may not be sent to the convenience store, in which case you may need to schedule a redelivery.

In the event you're not around when the package is delivered (which is highly likely if you're doing your job correctly and staying at the school until 5:00 pm) the postman will stick a missed delivery notification in your mailbox and give you an opportunity to pick it up or schedule a redelivery. Usually they will attempt to redeliver it at the same time the following day, which is a problem if you're not around. To reschedule a delivery, call the number on the bottom of the card left by the deliveryman. If you can't read Japanese and don't know how to reschedule a delivery, take the slip to your supervisor at the school and get them to help you.

Staying healthy and medicine

Staying healthy can be a bit of a challenge at times if you're not used to the Japanese diet. If you want to save money and not miss school days, don't get sick. It happens sometimes no matter what you do, but to increase the likelihood of staying healthy, be sure to eat lots of fish, vegetables, lay off the red meat and stay away from all the greasy foods when you cook. Be sure to stay away from people who are sneezing and coughing on trains and carry a small bottle of hand sanitizer.

Regarding medicine, if you need to get medicine look for any sign that says 薬屋 *Ku-su-ri-ya* (meaning drugstore) and you can find Japanese medicine there. There are also some stores in your area that won't have that exact phrase, but will use a similar kanji despite having a different name. When I was in Tokyo, my go-to drugstore was マツモトキヨシ *Matsumoto kiyoshi* since they also sold some of the necessary groceries needed such as laundry detergent, and shampoo.

While you can bring medicine from your home country, several drugs we normally have access to in America are in fact illegal in Japan. Certain stimulants (medicines that contain Pseudoephedrine, such as Actifed, Sudafed, and Vicks Inhalers) or codeine are prohibited if it contains more than the allowed quantity. According to Japanese law, up to a two-months' supply of allowable over-the-counter medication and up to two months' supply of allowable vitamins can be brought into Japan duty-free. Being caught in possession of illegal medicine and even trying to ship it from abroad can get you into legal trouble if you're caught, so just be aware. To be honest though, I have brought in some American medicines I needed by just simply putting them in my suitcase. The Japanese guards at the airport will likely just pass over it if they see a random box with English. From what I understood, mailing pharmaceutical drugs containing the illegal ingredients instead of bringing them in your suitcase is what has gotten people into trouble in the past.

Public schools and sick days

Depending on whether or not you're working in a private or public school, you may or may not have sick days outside of your holidays. Public school JETs have to sacrifice paid vacation days if they are sick even with a doctor's note. If you are sick and need to take time off from school, call anyone at your office up to the morning before your shift starts and you should be okay. If you run out of paid vacation days to sacrifice, and you start to lose the ability to come into the office 16 days a month, the school will start to deduct your salary.

Due to the system of only having a limited number of off days in a year, most Japanese teachers will bite the bullet and come into work even if they have the flu. Some of your co-workers will not tell people they have the flu and attempt to power through it because they also don't want to lose their vacation days. Although they mean well and don't want to hinder others, these types of actions are often the number one reason why illnesses spread around the office. If you do get sick, be sure to wear a surgical mask as you've likely seen other people have on your way to school. Not only is it polite, but wearing one around other sick people can supposedly reduce your chances of getting sick. As to how true this may be, I am not sure, but if you'd like to buy some surgical masks, you can get a decent sized pack at your local convenience store for around five dollars or less.

Food

In general, it is a good idea to cook more often than eat out, but how often you eat out will depend entirely on your food budget, where you live, how much money you're saving each month, or if you have student loans to pay. In addition to this formula, buying food and cooking it can be either more or less expensive depending on where you shop. In your first week I want you find the cheapest grocery store possible and shop there. Even if you choose the right store, be aware that some ingredients you really want are not going to be readily available due to price. For example, strawberries which would normally cost between $2.00 – $6.00 in America, will cost somewhere between $3.00 and $20.00 in Tokyo depending on where you go. It's all about finding the right supermarket for you. And yes, I've tried the $20.00 strawberries out of curiosity, and they were the exact same as the $3.00 ones you'd find at a smaller store. If you want cheap goods, I suggest you avoid underground grocery stores next to train stations. Those stores tend to overprice their goods since they can get away with it for being in a convenient location to customers. From my experience in Tokyo, there were two good chain stores to get relatively cheap food and they are located across Japan: Comodi iida and Life.

A popular Japanese grocery store. Food was great and affordable.

If you're in a college town they have lots of restaurants and hidden gems where you can eat a full meal for $5.00. Be sure to explore your area and if you make some Japanese friends, ask them for places you might want to visit and cheap places to eat. Ramen shops are good, but you shouldn't eat there every day, nor should you eat at American establishments unless you feel homesick. What I did was eat out once to twice a week, and then once a month at an American style restaurant when I wanted a taste of home. If I felt really homesick as I did in winter, I'd eat at an American restaurant two or three times a month.

Food Tip: Be sure to include enough money each month in your budget plus an additional $60.00 for a possible party with your co-workers. Due to my budget with student loans, I was only able to go half of the time, but your co-workers might want to go out for dinner after pay day. Join your co-workers for dinner if you can afford it. It's a great opportunity to get to know one another and just blow off some steam after a long month of work.

Taxes

Ah yes, everyone's favorite time of year. While I'm no expert on taxes, every year your community manager for whichever JET location you're in should send out an updated guide to dealing with taxes in Japan. What I can tell you however is this, you should be able to avoid double taxation and be exonerated from paying the federal income tax in the United States for up to two years. You may have to pay state taxes in your first year since you will not have been a resident in Japan long enough in your first year to be exempt, but by your second year, you should be able to prove you've been a resident long enough and avoid having to pay double taxes.

Every month a certain amount of your paycheck goes to your health insurance provided by your job, your pension, residence tax, and your taxes to the country. In March however you will get taxed twice since this is when the fiscal year in Japan ends. Since the government cannot wait for citizens to pay their March taxes in April, they apply the April taxes to your paycheck in March, so you're paying two months' worth of taxes during this time.

For a detailed guide on taxes, google the "Kumamoto Tax Guide for JETs".

Paying your utilities

All of your gas, water, and electricity bills will be sent to you in little slips with the word "important" *taisetsu* 大切 or "necessary" *hitsuyō* 必要 and PAYMENT DUE in big red English letters. Do not ignore these! Take the slips out and bring them to the convenience store because that is where you will pay them in cash. Go to any Lawson, Seven Eleven, or convenience store and you can bring your bills and pay them right there. The clerk will scan the barcode on the bill and you can pay it in cash. You might not be used to paying your bills in cash, but it's a nice luxury you'll miss if you ever go back to the United States.

51

Once you've paid your utilities, you might want to save the receipts for up to two months. I've seen this happen to a few JETs where the gas or water company calls up a JET claiming they did not pay their bills on time and that they will have their utilities turned off if they refuse to pay. Since my friends forgot to save their receipts of payment, they had to go to the store and have the shop clerk talk to the company to try and convince them they paid. To avoid having to deal with this mistake, save your utility payment receipts for up to two months and throw them out from there. Humans make mistakes, so be prepared if that happens.

Convenience stores

Japanese convenience stores are known for their wide variety of services and goods. You can do almost anything at a Japanese convenience store. You can...

- Withdraw or deposit money at an ATM
- Order concert tickets, convention tickets, art show tickets, museum tickets, movie tickets, amusement park tickets and instantly print them out
- Photocopy and scan documents and pictures
- Print documents
- Try new beverages yet to be in mass production
- Purchase an umbrella if it suddenly starts raining
- Get snacks at a cheap price and one-dollar to two-dollar rice balls that are refreshed daily
- Pickup packages you may have missed from a delivery when you were outside
- Get garbage bags / contact lens solution / toilet cleaners and toiletries
- Masks if you need them for when you're sick
- Comics
- Seasonal fried food or soups (known as oden) for $1-2.00
- Enter competitions
- Get a chance to instantly win a $5.00 - $10.00 worth of items if you spend $7.00 or more on a Sunday. You stick your hand in the box and pull out the coupon or whatever free item card you can get your hands on.
- City approved stickers you need in order to throw away furniture

- Fans for when it's hot
- Hand warmers during winter
- Alcohol and cigarettes of all different kinds (not endorsing it. Just stating a fact).
- Underwear, socks, shorts, and T-shirts in black and white.

Anything you can imagine; the convenience store can probably provide.

Post office awesomeness

Post offices can be really helpful in times of need. They typically operate the same way U.S. post offices do, but every ward in the cities should have a 24-hour post office window. If you need to ship some things home and you can't due to your work hours, don't fret. Ask your supervisor or someone you trust at the school to help you find the nearest 24-hour post office window (郵便局ゆうゆう窓口) pronounced as *yūbin kyoku yūyū madoguchi*. If you need to ship computer parts or anything fragile. You will have to ship it by air. Apparently, anything computer related including adaptors and batteries for some reason are prohibited on sea barges. Keep that in mind when you're making arrangements for leaving the country.

Winter and Summer and your apartment

To end this section, I'm going to talk about the winter, summer, and your apartment. Depending on your location, the apartments and buildings will be different. For example, due to heavy snowfalls and the common freezing temperatures in Hokkaido, the northern island of Japan, buildings are usually insulated and resistant to the cold. In other cities such as Tokyo, Osaka, and Kyoto, the apartment buildings are not well insulated since they have mild winters with the low temperature being 30 degrees and it is actually quite common for apartments to be rebuilt every 10 to 20 years. In other words, these buildings were not meant to last and were built light to also resist earthquakes. So, what does this mean?

Well imagine it's 30 degrees Fahrenheit outside and you're inside an apartment in Tokyo with limited insulation. You're likely going to feel very cold. The common apartment will have two rooms or even just one with a combined kitchen and living room / bedroom. You'll likely have a heater or air conditioner that operates on electricity, but even so it probably won't be that strong. When I was living in Tokyo, my apartment had a kitchen inside the hallway, a bathroom, and a living room / bedroom with a security shutter leading to the outside. It was fine for the summers since cool air could come through, but winter was awful. I could've gotten a space heater like most Japanese people, but my landlord was reluctant on me having a space heater operating on a wooden floor. A *kotatsu* could've worked, but my room was also small since I already had a desk and a full-sized bed plus a bookcase. So as a result, most of my apartment was about 35 degrees Fahrenheit during the winter months.

When choosing apartments make sure you have a room where you can isolate the heat if necessary. This is called "strategic heating." Thankfully my little built-in electric heater kept one room warm so I could retreat there for the night, but had I not had that ability to use strategic heating, I would've been in trouble. You can always use the electric heaters and air conditioners when necessary, but be aware that it can be expensive.

HEADS UP: The scenario I provided above was my own experience from the Tokyo apartments and talking with other JETs. Supposedly due to the extreme freezing temperatures in Hokkaido, all apartments there are required by law to be very well insulated, so you shouldn't have to worry about the cold too much there. Even if the apartments are well insulated, you shouldn't have to worry about the hot summers in Hokkaido since they're relatively mild compared to the average high 80-degree weather in Tokyo.

Chapter 3: The Office and You!

Day one and making a good first impression

If you're reading this you've most likely survived orientation without a hitch, got your apartment squared away and you're about to meet your supervisor and future co-workers. I'm sure you're brimming with excitement and eager to get started. I know I was too on the first day. First make sure to wear a suit and tie to your training the same day you meet your supervisor. You'll want to show you're serious about the job and nothing leads to a better first impression than dressing the part. The Japanese Teachers of English (JTEs) will be briefed on how to handle JETs in a separate room and hopefully you've been keeping in touch with them during your stay. If you haven't been keeping in touch with them or you're meeting them for your first time, that's perfectly fine. Depending on your supervisor's personality, they may or may not have contacted you earlier. On the day you meet your supervisor, a JET coordinator will gather all the JETs and their respective JTEs in a large room and they will call the Japanese teacher's name first and then your name so you both can meet in the center. It's kind of like a ceremony, so have fun and make the most of it. You can do one of several things depending on your relationship with the person. If you've been keeping in touch with them throughout your stay leading up to this moment, give them a hug. A lot of JETs did that and they hit it off well with their supervisor in their first meeting. You can also bow or give them a handshake. Whatever you do, keep in mind you'll likely be doing this in front of over 100 people, so greet your supervisor and do what makes you feel comfortable. Once you meet in the center, you're both free to head off to school.

Getting the lay of the land

After you arrive at the school the first place your supervisor will show you will likely be the faculty room. Make sure you bring water because the school is going to be hot. Japanese schools run on a very tight budget year-round, so the only places that will have some form of air conditioning will be the faculty room, principal's office, and the front office. I remember I didn't know this my first time around and I felt like I was going to faint due to the extremely high temperatures inside while wearing a business suit. Be prepared for a long hot day and pace yourself accordingly.

The structure and flow of a Japanese office will be different from what you're used to if you have teaching experience in the U.S. For starters, you won't have much personal space. Japanese faculty / staff rooms are divided in rows with a designated row for first-year teachers, second-year teachers, third-year teachers, student-affairs, general affairs, and IT. Unless you are on the end of a row, you will have a teacher sitting in front of you, behind you, and next to you on both sides. Thankfully all teachers in my school had a divider so they had some personal privacy from the person in front of them, but some schools may prohibit dividers, so check on that. While you won't have much in the way of personal space, you will have lots of chances to interact with teachers in your little section. It's great for building communities, but it can also be a real bummer if you don't get along with everyone in your immediate section. Finally, the vice principal will typically sit in the back with a view of everyone so he can call people to his desk, oversee their work, and keep an eye on things. The layout of the desks will make him appear like an overseer, but he means well.

Once your supervisor shows you your desk, have a seat and check it out. Ask questions when necessary and smile when you meet your vice principal. The vice principal holds a peculiar position of power since he is likely the hardest working, but sometimes the least appreciated. Any problems or issues a school faces go through him first while the principal is actually given public credit for any success the school achieves. In a way, the vice principal is really the person who runs the school from the inside while the principal is more of a public figure who signs documents and runs the occasional meeting and community event. Be sure to make a good impression on the vice principal by shaking his hand, bowing and speaking some Japanese, no matter how novice it may seem.

A great way to kick off your new work relationship is by saying: "*Hajimemashite, watashi wa (Name) to mōshimasu. Dōzo yoroshiku onegai itashimasu.*" 初めまして、私は（　　）と申します。どうぞよろしくお願いいたします。 "Hello my name is (your name). It's nice to meet you." The sentence ending *itashimasu* makes this a very formal greeting and I'm sure you will make a good impression if you try to speak the language. Depending on the vice principal's schedule he may take you on a tour of the school with your supervisor, so just go with the flow at this point, take an interest in what they say, smile, and have fun.

HEADS UP: You will likely have to switch into *uwabaki* 上履き or guest slippers upon entering the building. Don't worry. The shoes are most likely sanitized and they're safe to wear. This is common practice in Japan in order to prevent dirt from the street marking the school floors. You can put your shoes in a locker and then exchange the slippers back for them once you're done. This cultural phenomenon is why I suggested you bring two pairs of dress shoes. Do not feel like you have to wear these slippers year-round. You are more than welcome to wear your shoes. This way you can wear one pair indoors and another pair outside. If you'd like, you could commute in sneakers and then switch into dress shoes, but it's really up to you. Your students on the other hand will be wearing sneakers in the classroom. You can distinguish your students by the band on their shoes which will be red, green, or blue. If for example 3rd year students were wearing blue shoes in 2016, the incoming 1st years for 2017 would wear the blue shoes once the seniors have graduated. Japanese high schools and middle schools typically run for three years each and the color-coded shoes red, blue, green can be found in schools throughout the country, which leads me to believe this is a national practice.

After the tour, you'll likely be introduced to the principal. When you meet your principal, be sure to bow very low as that will show you are giving him great respect and that you feel honored to work for the school. This does not mean grovel and go on your knees as you see people do in samurai movies. This means to standup straight and then bow. To expose one's neck in Japanese society is a sign of respect and shows that you trust the person. A part of this tradition dates back to the samurai days when bowing to someone was the ultimate way of respect and trust, since you trusted in their character to not take out a sword and chop your head off. Back to reality though, before you leave the principal's office, present him the gift you prepared as a token of gratitude and appreciation for being given a chance to work at the school as a JET. Finally, as you're about to exit the office turn around and bow again and say *shi-tsu-rei-shi-masu* 失礼します which means "Pardon my intrusion. I take my leave."

Hopefully you're not tired yet on your already exciting and busy day, you got one more task ahead of you. Your supervisor will most likely take you to the front office where you will receive your first month's payment in cash and then some forms you will have to fill out for commuting, tax purposes, and depositing future payments into your bank account. If you haven't created your account yet, they will pay you in cash in an envelope. Tuck that envelope in your bag and guard it with your life until you get that bank account established. That's your first month's paycheck, so if that disappears, you're in trouble.

Work commuter pass

Before you leave the front office, make sure you have the proper form to get access to a commuter pass. A commuter pass will allow you to ride an unlimited amount of times from your nearest train station all the way to the train station at your office for a set price depending on the distance between the two stations. Commuter passes can last for a month, three months, six months, and a year. Getting this commuter pass will save you tons of money in the long run especially if you have a long commute. To get this pass, a member of the front office at your school will help you file the appropriate paperwork for you to take to the subway attendants. They'll file the paperwork and give you a commuter pass. After that though, you can combine that commuter pass to your normal commuter card used for traveling on buses, trains, and subways. This general commuter card is known as a Suica card and can be purchased for $5.00 at any station.

Once you've finished meeting the heads of your school and taking care of the administrative tasks, you'll be given a chance to sit back down in the teacher's room and hang out. Take the time to try and talk with teachers next to your desk and any who don't seem busy. If you have access to these tools at your new desk, take a pen and notepad and write your new colleagues' names. To help you memorize names ask your supervisor for an English copy of the seating chart. All schools should have a seating chart for visitors to refer to, so it shouldn't be too much trouble to ask for an English one so you can memorize names. If the school knows what they're doing, they will have prepared a desk for you in the teacher's office where you can sit and relax. Even if you tackle the administrative tasks early, you will not be dismissed until 5:00 pm, so relax. Talk to your fellow co-workers and your suitcase from the airport will likely arrive at the school so you can take it with you at the end of the day. On that note, congratulations! You survived day one.

Activate Sensei Mode – Daily schedule and flow

Entering the job as a JET provides some unique challenges starting within your first week. These challenges aren't bad, it's just simply a challenge. The issue is JETs arrive in August, meet the students and start working in September. You might think this is okay since that is how American schools and British schools operate, but Japanese schools actually begin in March. We're entering right in the beginning of the 2nd trimester so things are already underway, events have been scheduled, students and faculty already have established relationships, leaving you as the new teacher on the block.

That's okay. Think of this as an opportunity to provide a fresh perspective on Japanese school life and maybe even add some new energy to the work setting. Getting into the swing of things early will help you adjust quickly to your new environment. My advice is focus less on the stresses of a new job, and more on teaching your kids and getting along with people in the office. Let's walk through a typical day at the office from morning to night.

Wake up / your weekday morning

As a JET you're on the clock beginning at 8:30 am. You might think it's okay to waltz in at 8:15 am, but in reality, this means you should be at your desk by 8:00 am. The reason why is because you'll have to commute to school and allow for delays, put on your *uwabaki* or 2nd pair of shoes you'll leave in a designated locker, sign in, prepare your work materials for the day, answer any requests from teachers, attend the morning meeting and then rush to set up a classroom. Most likely you won't have to bear all of the above listed responsibilities in your first month, but be prepared to carry them out eventually. What helped me stay on track and focused throughout the year was a morning routine. I'd wake up at 5:45 am, shower, have a good breakfast, grab some coffee at my local Starbucks, catch up on news back home and then be on the train by 7:00 am in order to arrive at my school by

8:00 am. Sometimes if I wanted to participate in my school's morning basketball practices I would arrive at the school by 6:30 am, causing me to get up at 4:30 am and then shower in the athletic department's office before classes started.

Morning meetings

Once the chime rings at 8:30 am the vice principal will call a brief two to five-minute meeting in the teacher's room to make announcements or remind people of upcoming events. The morning meeting could be every day, or in my scenario once a week on Mondays. All of the teachers and administrators will gather in the staff room and talk about events happening for the week, emergency notices, requests, and reminders such as garbage pickup and other chores. First the vice principal will speak and pass it over to the principal. Then he will ask if the student administration, then disciplinary, then 1st years, 2nd years, 3rd years and anyone else if they want to add anything. If you want to say something at the end and only at the end you say "Hai" はい and then quickly say what you want to say in Japanese. Everyone is expected to be present for the meetings and if you don't show up, you'll be spoken to regarding your absence.

Bring on the classes

Once the morning meeting is over, you're going to see a rush of several homeroom teachers and administrators out the door. These faculty members either have a homeroom to manage for 10 minutes before the first class begins at 8:45 am or they have a meeting. Whatever you do, do not block the entrance to the door. Remain in your seat unless you have some place to go or a teacher to talk to. At this point, stay in your desk and prepare for your lessons or maybe just talk to a teacher who doesn't have lessons during first period.

My average class lasted about 50 minutes with a 10-minute break so teachers could go to the next room. Unlike the American system where students commute to classrooms, in Japan the teachers move from class to class while the students remain seated. When you teach you will move from class to class alongside the JTE and it is best to walk with them to try and solidify a good relationship. While you might want to go to the classroom ahead of the JTE to chat with students in English, from my experience it is best to only go when you have to set things up ahead of time. If you just go ahead of the JTE to the classroom it prevents you from helping the JTE should they happen to forget an item at the last minute or if they're carrying too many books or handouts for the class. You also run the risk of the students accidentally viewing you as their peer when you're not entering with the JTE and it invites them to perhaps ask questions they normally wouldn't ask otherwise. In short, walk with your JTE to the classroom and offer help when you can. If you need to set up the classroom ahead of time or in the rare event the students and the teachers move to a new room due to a location change, then act accordingly.

NB: The rooms are subje

Department	1	2	3	4	5	6	1	2
Career Guidance	3-3Ecv 3-3CR	3-5Ecv 3-5CR	3-4Ecv 3-4CR		1-1ECI 1-1CR		1-1ECI 1-1CR	3-4E 3-4C
General Affairs	1-5ECI 1-5CR	2-2ECII 2-2CR		2-3ECII 2-3CR		2-6EEI 2-6CR	M	
Career Guidance	3-4ECII 3-4CR			3-1Ecv 3-1CR			M	3-2E(3-2C
Homeroom 2-5				2-4ECII 2-4CR	2-5ECII 2-5CR	2-3EEI 2-3CR		2-2EEI 2-2CR
Student Guidance				3-1Ecv 3-1CR	2-3EEI 2-3CR	2-6EEI 2-6CR	2-2EEI 2-2CR	
homeroom 3-6	3-3Ecv 3-3CR	3-5Ecv 3-5CR	3-4Ecv 3-4CR		3 DE	3 DE	3-6ECII 3-6CR	3-4E 3-4C
homeroom 1-2	1-6ECI 1-6CR				1-2ECI 1-2CR	1-7ECI 展開3	1-2ECI 1-2CR	IS
homeroom 1-4	1-5ECI 展開3				1-12ECI 展開3	1-7ECI 1-7CR	1-12ECI 展開3	
JET*	1-6ECI 展開3				1-2ECI 1-2CR		1-1ECI 1-1CR	
ALT*								
ALT*								

The JET* works 16 days per month. The workdays for the next m
The ALTs* are assigned classes according to the contracts made.

My old Monday schedule with six periods.

After the 4th period is usually lunch. Everyone's school is different during this hour. Some schools have a community dining hall or lunchroom where faculty and students eat together. Other schools require the homeroom teacher to eat lunch inside the classroom with students, while in other schools

61

like mine the teachers eat in the faculty room and give students privacy to eat by themselves. You will have 45 minutes to eat lunch and start preparing for the next activity if you have a class beginning 5th period. But you can relax. Hang out with the people in your section and try talking to them. If your section isn't very talkative and you have no meetings or anything planned, walk throughout the school and chat with students.

What I did was keep a little whiteboard and wrote where I was. If I was at the library, I would write "library" or "wandering the halls" in Japanese. This way if teachers or students needed to get a hold of me, they could write a post it note and leave it on my board so I'd see it when I returned. When I did manage to find time to chat with students, I always kept it brief, maybe one or two minutes. After all the students are trying to relax and recuperate from 4th period. We were in their shoes too once, and I'm sure you can understand their desire to want to talk with their friends rather than a teacher. Respect their privacy and chat with them, but keep it within limits.

5th and 6th period will tend to go by either really quickly or really slowly. If your students just came back from gym, they're going to be tired and will most likely not want to participate. If it's 6th period and especially if it is Friday, your students will be anxious, and likely say "*hayaku owarō.*" 早く終わろう "Let's finish early." Try not to take offense, and either use the energy to your advantage or try to keep things calm. After classes the homeroom teachers will return to their homerooms and make announcements and address any issues that occurred for about 10 minutes. Once that's over, afterschool activities begin.

Afterschool

Once 2:30 hits and homeroom ends, the major part of your work day is finished. Most teachers run off to their respective club activities and the vice principal and principal will attend meetings with various departments. Often times there may be all-faculty meetings, which by the way…you do not have to attend. This is one of the times where it pays to be a JET because by having you remain in the teacher's room, faculty members can run back and retrieve forgotten items and documents without having to borrow the key from their boss. You're also spared from long moments of silence in meetings while people reflect and take several minutes and sometimes hours to make a decision. You'll also often find other people falling asleep in the back of the room during these meetings so you're not missing much.

Keep in my mind though, your actions all depend on the kind of image you want to represent and what the school faculty will permit. If you want to be considered a full-fledged Japanese faculty member, you might want to attend the meetings. But believe me when I say this, you're in for a real sleeper if you don't know Japanese. This could also lead to the teachers giving you more responsibilities than you're ready to handle without proper training.

During afterschool you have a few options and this will also be a time when your actions will be looked upon and judged. You can sit at your desk all day and twiddle your thumbs and make lessons which may or may not be accepted. Or you can get off your butt and participate in various club activities or even walk around the classrooms and strike up conversations with students. I prefer the latter because it shows you care about the students, you're wanting to get involved in the community, and you are willing to expose students to foreign culture and cooperating with someone from a foreign country.

When I was a JET, I offered my services and time to work with the boys' basketball team. I loved playing basketball in high school and despite my lack of skills, they welcomed me since I was able to allow the team to have full 5 on 5 practices. I tried to strike a balance between helping them and working on my lessons. Practices were on Mondays, Tuesdays, Thursdays, Fridays, and an occasional weekend practice. Four times a week I played basketball and then over time my schedule changed. I discovered the girls' basketball team needed people, so I volunteered with another teacher to coach and spend time with the girls. Then I was requested to rebuild a former English club so I spent time with them and by the end of my time as a JET, I was doing three different clubs four days a week and took Wednesday to work on my lessons. The times I spent with the club members were some of my favorite moments as a JET and they even threw me a farewell basketball game at the end as a thank you for my hard work and services.

My point here is that participating in different aspects of the school can really pay off and show that you're willing to take the initiative. The JETs who typically stay only for a year are the ones who don't try to get too involved. I understand being shy can make things difficult, but ask your supervisor for help and see if they can arrange for you to help out a club.

HEADS UP: If the school's club activities meet on weekends, be sure to tell the coach and the students that you cannot make all of the weekend practices due to your contract. While you probably can make the practices, I want you to carve a social life outside of the school. If you have some JTEs who make your life a living hell, you'll thank me for this advice later. It's also just a nice mental break from being at the school 24/7. You're living in a foreign country for a limited time, so you should try to make the most of it.

School year work and schedule

Unlike American schools where schools close from June to August, the Japanese school system works year-round almost daily. There are many differences so I'll start highlighting them here. First the school year begins in March and ends in April. So that means as soon as graduation ends, the opening ceremony for incoming students starts within two weeks. One could compare the Japanese school system to a well-oiled machine that keeps churning students in and hopefully adults out. Summer vacation only lasts three weeks in August, and teachers are required to stay in the office. The summer work requirement is a bit of a downside to the job, but there are already several holidays throughout the school year, so it's not too bad.

This seemingly never-ending schedule will be a little weird at first and you might think you need to be doing something all the time, but you don't. All you have to do is stick to your contract. You are required to work 16 days each month from 8:30 am until 5:00 pm. Once 5:00 pm hits, you're off the clock and you're free to do as you wish. However, if you want to leave a good impression on your co-workers, bosses, and fellow students, I recommend you stay until 5:45 pm or 6:00 pm, especially if you live close by. I lived 45 minutes away, so I had an excuse, but I often tried to stay afterwards in the beginning. Now I do say you're required to work 16 days, but due to the calendar system and when your contract begins, you may be required to work 17 days during the month of August after your first year. Do not get upset. Just go with the flow.

Before each month begins, you will be required to choose which days you come in, and I highly suggest you choose the days when you're scheduled to teach. While you could schedule some of your work days to be when you don't teach, that is irresponsible. For example, in the beginning I was teaching on Monday, Tuesday, Thursday, and Friday. While I could've made some of my work days on Wednesdays, that would've been inconsiderate of the other teachers' work schedules. What will most likely happen is you'll schedule the 16 days on your work days and due to a school event or a national holiday, you'll have the opportunity to take a normal work day off. The work schedule is manageable as long as you stay healthy and meet everyone's demands.

How to network with colleagues and get along with everyone

Phase 1: Okay so flash forward to the first day of school. You've most likely "briefly" met most of the faculty if not everyone. You're expected to give your intro lesson in just a few days after students take their return exams after break, and you're now wondering "How are you going to get along with everyone?" "Will the students like me?" "What is my job again and why did I come here?" Fear not my friends, my goal in this section is to help you get along with most people and to make the most of your time as a JET.

The first thing you want to do if you haven't already is give a gift to the big three: your supervisor, vice principal, and principal for hiring you. This is a thank you gift and a good way to win them over to your side and open the door for questions you may have about the school and what they want you to accomplish during your time in Japan. Once you do that, it's time to work on what I like to call: The Name Game. Hopefully you've received by now the name list of all of the teachers in your area and you'll probably be sitting next to an English teacher. Be sure to remember the names of all of the teachers sitting in your immediate area (your row) and try to talk to them. If you don't know Japanese and they don't know English, just start by saying hello. The teachers are often really busy during the beginning of the semester, so the ideal time to talk to them is during lunch breaks or afterschool if their club isn't meeting and they're just killing time.

What's important about this mission is that I don't want you to rely on your English teacher / supervisor to translate everything you say in order to make connections. The reason why is because **1. The English teacher may be self-conscious of their English skills in front of colleagues, and believe me this happens a lot. 2. The English teacher has issues and problems of their own, especially if they're a homeroom teacher.** You need to grow up a little bit and not rely on them for help the entire time. I know this may not seem fair, but use a phrasebook if you don't have anything and just try to communicate. While some people focus on passing out treats to all of the teachers on day one, this isn't obligatory and in my opinion your time is better focused on trying to establish a meaningful connection with the colleagues around you.

You might be saying to yourself, "Talking is all well and good, but what if I don't know any Japanese?" Well if that's the situation, start by saying hello and begin to study Japanese in your spare time. Grab a Japanese book or phrasebook and start studying before school, during your breaks and a little bit after club activities. I mean think about it, you're in a foreign country surrounded by people who probably would like to talk to you, but they most likely lack the communication skills to do so and they're way too busy to learn English. It's up to you to strike up a conversation, put yourself out there and study the Japanese language. Most people will be pleased you're putting in the effort since it shows respect on your part and that you want to be accepted by the community. Be sure to push yourself by learning five new words each day and trying something new on your fellow teachers in their spare time. Even if it seems brief, they will be happy. And if anyone makes fun of your accent or is just a jerk saying you don't need to study Japanese, ignore them. They're not worth your time getting angry or flustered. Yes, you will meet those types as well, but just be yourself and you'll win people over.

Phase 2: Now that you've been studying Japanese for a while (two or three weeks), try to bring in a snack every two weeks or so to share with your immediate section or the people sitting around you. Everyone's blood sugar starts to drop at around 3:00 pm or a little before, so if you can bring in a snack to share with everyone they'll really appreciate it. Passing out little snacks was common practice in the sections at my school and it will show you care and are picking up on the little traditions amongst your teachers. Be sure the teachers are actually passing out snacks before you attempt this though. Hopefully by this time you're on good terms with most of the people in your section, and now it's time to check back on the vice principal and principal.

Whenever you see the principal in the hallways, keep the conversation brief and smile and always ask how he's doing. For the vice principal, if you want to stay on his good side, always arrive to work early and sign in. I remember when my school received a new vice principal, we had a bit of a spat. One day I was late by 30 minutes due to a technical problem on one of the trains. My new vice principal whom I had only known for about a month was pissed. I had to submit a form explaining why I was late, and then show online that the train was in fact delayed and that I wasn't lying. Eventually we got on good terms, but good grief if you want to stay in everyone's good graces...**NEVER BE LATE TO ANYTHING IN JAPAN!**

HEADS UP: Being late in Japan is like the cardinal sin. The way the Japanese view tardiness is much more extreme compared to your home countries. They might say "Oh it's okay, don't worry about it." But to the Japanese they were raised to judge people's characters based on tardiness and keeping one's word. To them, being late shows that you don't care enough about them and their personal lives. As one of my colleagues advised me when I got chewed out by my boss and I was confused as to why when it wasn't my fault, he said "you should've considered the possibility of someone dying on a train, having a heart attack, starting a fight, freak storm, or just about anything. That's why so many Japanese people arrive to work really early, because they prepare for events like this. They want to leave a good impression on their boss and prepare for the worst-case scenario." What I learned from this experience: *__As a general rule of thumb, always arrive 30-45 minutes early to work and just prep for the day__*. When the first homeroom bell rings, you should be at your desk or preparing a lecture room in advance.

Phase 3: Now that you've hopefully been staying on good terms with your supervisor, JTEs, vice principal, principal, and nearby teachers, it is now time to expand and reach out to the other teachers outside of your department. My advice for this is to try and startup a conversation with one teacher per day and spend 5 minutes to just try and talk to them in the office when they look bored and have nothing better to do. Just focus on one teacher per day and I bet you'll start seeing results sooner than you realize. If you don't feel comfortable doing this, I understand. Meeting new people can be tough at times when you have no real connection or need to engage them, but the more people you know and can get along with, the easier your job will be in the long run. What I did to engage people was host a work party, known as an *enkai*. Myself with the help of another teacher took a week to plan the event and we invited a mix of colleagues we knew liked each other, but whom I also wanted to develop a connection with.

Work enkai

Who doesn't like a little bit of work/life balance? Am I right? The Japanese are known for a couple of things. From their hard work ethic, strict beliefs, to their drinking games, and *enkais*. An *enkai* 宴会 is an after work-drinking party where co-workers get together to relax, maybe vent their frustrations and gossip about work and forget some of the problems they have at home. There are occasions where even the boss will join the festivities, but don't count on him attending every *enkai*. The *enkais* are where the drinking and fun culture of Japan really shine and I encourage you to take part in them as long as you have the finances to participate and get a ride back home.

If your school is decent towards you, your co-workers will most likely invite you to an *enkai* within your first few weeks on the job to welcome you. There are a few tips I'd like to share so you can get the most out of the experience.

1. Only drink as much as you feel obligated to. Don't ever feel peer pressured to drink. For the first *enkai*, you are viewed as a guest.

2. Whatever happens at the *enkai*, stays at the *enkai*. Did someone puke all over a co-worker and confess their love for her while sobbing? I don't know, it didn't happen. If it did happen, no one talks about it at the office the next day. The personalities and stories shared and experienced at *enkai*s are separate from office hours. Make sure you don't bring up anything embarrassing the following day.

3. Don't bad mouth your principal or boss. It's okay to ask for advice on dealing with a student or any issues you have, but don't insult someone or start a rumor. You're not in high school anymore and this is not the United States. Save the gossip for when you meet with other JETs or Skype with your family. Yes, this does mean I'm holding you to higher standards than your co-workers, but this is because you'll likely not yet know where you stand in the social hierarchy at work, and the last thing you need is a rumor or complaint you said to come back and bite you.

HEADS UP: Depending on the nature of the *enkai* and the reason for holding it, teachers may be expected to give speeches. You may also be asked to give a speech. Just go with the flow. These could be what you enjoyed about school or a particular event that just took place. On another note, the teachers jokingly call these events *hanseikai*, 反省会 (meaning meetings of reflection) when students are nearby. This is so the students do not attempt to follow the teachers to the bar or restaurant after school. Other terms for an enkai are *nomikai, nomyunication* which is a play on two words: *nomu* 飲む, to drink and communication コミュニケーション to communicate.

School events

The Summer Carnival

Your school will have many events throughout the year and it is best if you mark these events on your calendar once you arrive. The biggest events for a school are usually the summer festival which lasts an entire weekend and takes one to three days to prepare. The summer festival is where each classroom from the first years to third years take a role and organize an event. For example, in my school, 1st year classes were divided up and given a theme to present at a talent show or dance performance. 2nd year students were in charge of a haunted house, a carnival games area, and a picture booth, while 3rd year students were in charge of selling cakes, mini hotdogs, chocolate, and frozen icies. The sports clubs such as basketball will also host a rival school and play in a game. Hopefully they win, because it's a slap in the face if they lose. Dance clubs and other clubs will perform and host booths and events during the festival. It's absolute chaos and a lot of fun, but in the end, everyone has a good time, and memories are made. After the celebrations the teachers almost always throw an *enkai* since the following Monday is a holiday, so make sure you get in on the celebrations.

Ways you can participate and get involved are to ask teachers what they might need for help. Ask students if they need help painting or just try to start up an English conversation with some students. I know for a fact they'll be thrilled the new JET is giving them attention and they'll get free English practice. Just make sure your lesson prep for the following week is finished and that all of the teachers know what is going in your next class after the holiday weekend.

On the day of the festival, let your supervisor know that you want to take photos so parents don't think you're some kind of oddball photographing their children. My school required us to inform the principal if we wanted to take photos, but they relaxed that rule in my 2nd year. Next is to participate in as many events as possible, but my advice is to visit the events hosted by your club group and your 1st year students (presuming you mainly teach them). By showing your support, it shows that you care about your students' wellbeing and that you want them to succeed. It also gives them bragging rights that the new JET came to their booth.

Sports Day

The next event you should be paying attention to is Sports Day which is usually held after the welcome ceremony in mid-spring. The school divides the classes into three or four groups so 1st years, 2nd years, and 3rd years have a chance to work together. Sports Day usually begins with a dance competition. The dance is judged by a few teachers and you may even be asked to judge. These dances are great to watch because students make their own outfits and flags, and perform in a loud chorus. It kind of reminds one of a war chant, but with synchronized movements. Afterwards the teams participate in a variety of events such as tug of war, relay races, and the human chariot.

HEADS UP: Please note that the dance has its style originating from WWII. This was confirmed by several teachers I spoke to after the event. There is a salute in the dance that looks as though students are saluting Adolf Hitler, but don't worry about that. Please don't take offense.

It's just an old tradition that looks similar to the salute. The students do not mean any ill intent towards anyone.

The human chariot is quite an experience. When my school did this, only the boys were allowed to participate due to the violent nature of the game. Each of the three teams will have around four or five squads with each squad consisting of four members. One carries the hat grabber on his shoulders while the other two support the hat grabber by holding their feet. The goal of the hat grabber is to wrestle and steal as many hats from opposing squads. These squads are usually attacking and running away from each other at high speeds, so you can imagine things get quite physical really quick. Don't worry though, this sport is quite common in Japanese high schools and while accidents do happen, everyone usually has a good laugh. This is actually one of the most anticipated events of the day because it demonstrates the physical strength of the boys and provides them bragging rights at the beginning of the school year, especially if a first-year student team wins the match.

The final event before the scores of all the teams are tallied up is the relay race. Typically, it is a mix of 1st, 2nd, and 3rd years against the teachers. The idea is to let the students win and have some fun, so don't worry or take it too seriously. At my school all of the teachers dressed up in ridiculous Halloween outfits. It was great, so just focus on running your heart out and smile. Win or lose, you'll have a good experience to talk about at the following *enkai*.

Graduation

Graduation is by far one of the most important events at the school. It's a time where third year students say goodbye and teachers who have worked for years also say their farewells. If your school isn't strict, they will seat you with the other teachers and allow you to watch the proceedings. Usually the ceremony begins with a speech by the principal, then everyone sings the Japanese national anthem: Kimi Ga Yo, a depressing song from WWII. Then the vice principal speaks, the head of the parent student committee speaks, the principal speaks and gives out last-minute awards to outstanding students. The band will then perform a song or two while the diplomas are passed out. Once all students take their seats, the principal ends with a heartfelt speech about the message he wants students to take with them as they enter the adult world. You know how it is, and we've all seen this at least twice in our lifetimes back home. Although graduation is nothing new to us, being able to watch the graduation ceremony is a sensitive topic of discussion in the JET community. You may encounter some problems regarding the politics of graduation during your adventure in Japan. I will explain why in the upcoming problems section, but please bear with me.

Welcome ceremony

After graduation and spring break the next round of students will be welcomed into the school and there will be a lot of pomp and circumstance throughout the day. The welcome ceremony is similar to the graduation ceremony, but shorter and not as important in my opinion. Everyone gets dressed up so be sure you're wearing a suit and tie or a nice business outfit. At the ceremony, the students follow their homeroom teachers in rows and march to the gym. They sit down, the class representative makes a heartwarming speech about what they hope to experience in high school, the vice principal and principal make speeches alongside the parent association, and that's about it. While I was allowed to sit and watch the welcome ceremony, I was mainly benched during the day. There are no classes for the JET to teach and the teachers take a half day to acquaint themselves with the students and pass out syllabus before the day ends. Honestly, if you have the ability to schedule your work days, you could skip the welcome ceremony and not be penalized for it. If you really want to attend, you can try to make a case for it, but honestly, you're not missing much. On this day, the stars of the show are the first-year homeroom teachers, the principal and vice principal.

Sick days

This subject gets brought up every year in JET forums and gatherings. I have good news for you if you're in a private school. You will most likely have the ability to take sick leave and have it not affect your vacation time. If you're a public school JET, you get no compensation if you take sick leave and yes it will reduce your vacation time. If you think about complaining, all I can say is "Welcome to Japan! Where overwork is a national problem and people do commit suicide over it." Yes, it is dark, but it's just the culture and work ethic of teachers here. I remember when I was taken aback by the sick leave system for public school JETs. One day in late February, I could barely stand and felt nauseous and since I wasn't scheduled to teach that day anyway due to exams, I thought I could take the day off. When I phoned my co-worker, she warned me that it was okay to take sick leave, but that I would lose vacation time as a result of it. As a JET we are only granted 10 days of paid vacation time in our first year after working for 80% of the work days during our first six months. If you've been hoping to return home or visit a special location and you've already made plans, you can bet you'll feel obligated to march into school to avoid ruining your plans you've made with family and friends.

You might think, "but I'm actually sick and it's not fair!" Well you're right, it's not fair and your boss and co-workers will not care. To them especially if they are the traditional type, they view sickness as being the fault of the person who is sick since they believe it could've been avoided had the person taken proper care of themselves. I know I'm casting the

Japanese in a negative light with this description, but this attitude and belief still resides with the older generation as it did with my supervisor. While your co-workers may say "it's okay. Don't worry about it." They will be upset to a certain degree because that means someone will have to take care of the work you've failed to show up for, and they don't view it as fair when you take the easy way out while most of them march and 頑張る *"ganbaru"* or "persevere" through the work day.

Taking holidays when you really shouldn't, was a small problem I had to deal with at my job. I remember when I had some co-workers turn on me and harass me for just attending my cousin's wedding in America. Things eventually returned to normal, but here is what I want you to remember. What most JETs fail to realize in the beginning is how you'll be treated as a guest during the first three months, but after that your co-workers and boss will expect you to acclimate to the culture and their workflow. There will be no special exceptions for you because you're a foreign visitor, and you must be ready to make some sacrifices. If you're not ready to do just that without facing some consequences, I don't recommend you take this job or if you do, only stay one year. The attitudes towards you taking time off outside of holiday seasons will depend on the culture of your workplace, but be prepared for the possibility of a little backlash.

If you really want to get along and not disturb the peace at work, I recommend only taking 年休 *nenkyū* or paid leave if you're absolutely forced to by the school nurse. If they take your temperature and force you to stay at home, then you won't lose an entire day's worth of paid vacation and they'll be less likely to penalize you for it. Only use your paid vacation in combination with when the school is out of session so you can technically extend the holidays you already have and make the best use of them. For example, a common technique during the summer holidays is to take the following Monday off after the last day of classes on Friday. When I was a "guest" during my first three months, they allowed me to rearrange the schedule in the event I became sick which was only for one day. After that they wouldn't let me since I had paid vacation and I was treated as a normal employee.

How school fits into society and your role as a sensei

As a sensei you are held to great expectations by Japanese society. A sensei is not just your standard teacher who is in charge of ensuring the children know how to multiply, divide, know the names of all the prefectures and who founded Tokyo after the capital moved from Kyoto. As a teacher in Japanese society you are held to be a model citizen who is in charge of raising the children of society and instilling the values of human decency where the parents failed to teach their children. You are viewed as a second parent.

Here's an example from my school. A child was caught stealing from a grocery store next to the school and was punished by the school and reprimanded. The parents were summoned into the school to handle discipline and work on an agreement on how to approach the situation. The only problem was, the parents saw no obligation or duty to educate their child on the matter. In the parents' mind, it was the responsibility of the school and particularly the homeroom teacher to handle any problems their children faced while attending school. Any discipline problems you may face in class, while possibly the result of poor parenting, are blamed on you and the staff.

While there are some cons to being viewed as a second guardian to the children of the nation, there are some perks that go with it. If you mention you're a teacher in social outings, you are often held with great respect by the community for being trusted to educate the youth of Japan. I've even gotten a discount at a store or two when just answering a question in casual conversation that I was a teacher at a local high school. Another benefit is that the police, will not stop you if you prove you are a teacher. The downside however is that if you're caught or involved in any negative televised incident, you will be attacked by society, the JET program will be to blame, and your school will have to summon the principal to appear on your behalf on national television and bow in apology for their mistake in hiring you. This was the kind of story told to us at orientation, and while our instructor may have possibly exaggerated some of the details to scare us, with the way society is, it wouldn't surprise me if most of it were true. If you do your job and act normal, everything will be fine and you'll have a great time. Most importantly, treat every day as if you're representing your country and one of the most respected members of society.

So far, you've likely won over the heart of your principal, vice principal, supervisor, and the teachers sitting around you and perhaps your students. You're also probably maintaining a good attendance record due to the advice I gave you. But there are certain things and customs around the office you should be aware of.

Your school's mission and how to get involved

Each school in Japan has a different purpose in mind and thus it is your goal to figure out how you fit into the equation and how you can make the most of your time as a JET. There are some examples such as elite test prep schools, night schools for delinquents, private schools with a focus on English, and low-level high schools whose purpose is to contain the students and get them to finish school without getting expelled (my specialty). Let's go through each school really quickly.

Elite test prep schools: These are the schools whose purpose is to get their students to progress to Tokyo University, a.k.a. the Harvard University of Japan. In the worst-case scenario, some teachers are paid more based on how many individual students from their classes they send to Tokyo University or any top tier school. In my opinion, this is a tough JET placement because teachers are so focused on getting their students to pass the college entrance exams, that they won't have time to try anything experimental in the classroom.

In this scenario your best bet is to study what books the school is using for English and design exercises you can prove will help the students' understanding of the target grammar. While this may seem robotic at times, some students will have a very high-level of English, so it will make for great conversations about politics, business, and world affairs outside of class. These students will surprise you and will be hungry for conversation between classes, so be sure to nurture them. You might want to talk with teachers in what they would like you to do to help them in achieving their goals. If you feel like you're not getting enough time in the classroom, talk to students between classes.

Language schools: Some of the higher-level schools focus on language learning and studying abroad. This is the perfect environment for a JET, especially one with formal teaching experience because they will have the best chance to experiment in the classroom and convince students to study abroad. In this scenario I would suggest focusing heavily on building a language club or contributing to a club where English can be used. You could work on contests to promote study abroad, and even make a debate team as some of the more fortunate JETs did in their free time. Whatever you do, try to strike a balance however between English grammar and conversation. The kids get enough drills and boring grammar work in the classroom, so try to give them some reprieve from the monotony of textbook English. Of course, you will have to listen to the teachers in charge of the club, but you might just be lucky enough to run it yourself like I did.

You could also organize parties during the holiday seasons of Halloween, Thanksgiving, Christmas, etc. If you really want to develop a stronger bond with students who wish to study more English, you could offer private lessons afterschool. This is a wonderful idea, but beware of the time sink this could trap you in. One of the best JETs I met at my post development conference ran 1-on-1 conversation lessons and catered to those who wanted test prep for the speaking portion of entrance exams and also those who just wanted to get better at colloquial English. You'll need to treat everyone fairly and do your best to not be overwhelmed. Remember, legally you are only required to work until 5:00 pm and anything after that is volunteer work at the risk of your health and time. Think wisely before you take the plunge.

On another note, I wouldn't meet with any individual student more than once or twice a week. If you do, regardless of your gender, there is a possibility of being accused of a sexual relationship or even a homosexual relationship. Due to America's increasing relaxed standards towards marriage and the freedom to choose one's partner, some people in Japanese society are wary of us as teachers even if it is a student of the same gender. A few of my fellow JETs encountered this misunderstanding during their times in Japan, so be sure to set some boundaries and know what you're getting into.

Difficult schools: You're at a difficult school where a majority of students dislike English and most of the teachers have given up on the students due to delinquency, or because they dislike their jobs. This was unfortunately my scenario. Any attempts I made to do extra things in English after school were met with resistance from time to time (even my private lessons 1 on 1). There is a chance some of the teachers you'll be working with are going to be placed there as punishment. One of my coworkers admitted to me that he was forced to teach at my school as punishment for punching another student in a former school. Later in the year, two other teachers were dismissed due to unknown reasons. One day they just stopped showing up to work.

The students at this type of school are most likely from troubled neighborhoods where their families live in low-income housing and a parent abandoned them. This was a common scenario amongst the students I taught. As a result, they had little schooling in the ways of manners and often times their attention span was short. Discipline problems were rampant in the school and most lessons were difficult to teach. You'll likely not have a perfect JET experience here, but you can make the most of it.

First, participate in as many club activities as possible. What you'll be doing first is scouting students who are interested in speaking with you and then trying to make a positive impact on their lives. You may lose the classroom battles, but in club activities, as long as you're a positive influence and not distracting, you can win some of the students over. That's what I did in basketball club and dance club for a bit.

Next, do your best to create an English club that is fun and focused on teaching topics the students won't get in the classroom such as slang and colloquial sentences. The truth is most of the English lessons at the school will be very low- level using books where the text is 36 size-font and maybe three to four sentences per page. Give students a fun challenge where they will be learning things they can use in class and outside of it and you'll get repeat students. When I made the English club at school, we started with seven members and grew to 16 and then ended at nine once the seniors graduated. It was a fun club and everyone felt welcome and in a safe space. It was successful because it was one of the few things some my students looked forward to every week, the chance to learn a new language with people across different grades in a welcoming environment.

The challenge of being a JET

Here is the truth and it is going to be sad to hear if you're one of the rosy teachers hoping to be the next Yamaguchi Kumiko and change your school as you see in Japanese School soap operas. The truth is, English education is not as valued in Japanese middle or high schools compared to math and science. If you want a good comparison, think back to when you were learning French, Spanish, or Latin in your high school days. You probably had to take it as a requirement to "broaden your horizons" and your teacher was enthusiastic about it, but in reality, you probably didn't care. In fact, you probably looked at the back of the workbook for the answers so you could just finish your homework early. If that's not you, then kudos, you're not the norm.

The most important skills valued for the college entrance exams in Japan are math, science, essay writing, and history. English is not so much a requirement and it mainly applies to those interested in language schools and even then, the tests are primarily written and the speaking portion of the test is a joke by most professional speakers. Trust me, I actually prepped a couple of the students for the second highest level, and it was a cakewalk. If you think about it, you've just become the equivalent of your former high school's language teacher. Not every person you meet is going to be excited about studying English, no matter how hard you try to motivate them. This is a truth you need to accept. What will happen though, is you'll have a small group of students who want to learn English and share your culture, and that small group is who you should be focusing on.

What really helps when you're a JET is to celebrate the small victories. If you believe that every student is going to speak fluent English by the time you leave and you'll revolutionize the education system, I'm sorry but you're delusional. Your colleagues will likely consider you naïve as they did with me in the first two months until I wised up and understood the situation. Everyone has different goals, but set yourself up for success with small goals and you'll be much happier. Before you start planning anything drastic, get a lay of the land and try to understand your school's culture and place in society. For example, is your school a technical school where English is viewed as just a "filler course" in the curriculum? Is your school a private high school focusing on languages and getting students to study abroad? Is your school a lower tier school where the students are thankful to just get a job at a fast food restaurant upon graduation? By knowing your school's culture and ideology, you'll be able to establish better goals everyone can benefit from and better understand your position in the hierarchy.

You're not always welcome

The other aspect of the JET program I want you to consider is that while you're a "guest" and the program is a bridge between Japan and outside countries, you will not be welcome some of the time. You might be thinking "WHAT?!?! WHY? I'VE DONE NOTHING WRONG!" It's true, you personally haven't done anything wrong, it is merely the circumstances in which you were brought into the school that may pose a problem for some people.

Imagine this scenario: you are a highly distinguished faculty member at your high school who has taught for more than 20 years. You know how to run a classroom - your students love you year-in and year-out and you've recently received an award for your outstanding teaching. Life couldn't get any better than this. One day you walk into the office to hear about an exchange program between your country and a foreign country where the foreign instructor must team teach with you. Perhaps you're intrigued at the thought of it, but you may also likely feel uncomfortable. You might even ask yourself, "Why do I have to teach with another instructor from a foreign country when I'm already a good teacher? What did I do wrong? This isn't fair! Just because that country won a war 50 years ago doesn't mean they can force me to share my classroom with an upstart teacher who likely doesn't have experience in the field."

Now back to my main point in this section, I want you to remember this. ***You're entering the territory of already established teachers who have their own methods and who will most likely and should outrank you in skill and experience.*** I don't care if you got a Bachelors or Masters degree in teaching from Harvard and neither does anyone at the school. Your partner in the classroom has probably had more field experience. No matter what happens, do not say "Mr. / Mrs. Yamagawa doesn't know how to teach. This isn't how we do it in America or my home country! Jeez no wonder every Japanese person's English sucks!" You have no right to say that. Sorry to be harsh, but as a visitor to the school, you will need to take into consideration how each teacher feels about your presence. I recommend talking about the JTEs' attitudes towards the program with your supervisor. This way you'll be less likely to offend people going into the classroom. Believe me, I wish I had done this in my first month and had known that my presence wasn't welcomed at first. In the end I fixed most of those issues, but it took a while.

Throughout my time as a JET, I encountered scenarios ranging from the awkward to what was considered borderline harassment and disruptive to my job. This wasn't just me however, I noticed that almost every JET at the post development conference faced as least some kind of cultural problem or misunderstanding. It was my experience hearing the stories of other JETs that inspired me to write a large portion of this book in the hope that it would help others and save time and frustration. The goal of this next section is not to bash Japan or its citizens in any way. But rather to compile a list of problems JETs faced and how they resolved them. If this section can provide some insight into any problem you're facing no matter how weird it is, then I've done my job. I love Japan and I plan to visit for many more years to come. If anything, I hope this section will give you confidence that you will be able to effectively counter and deal with any situation you might experience and then grow from it as a teacher and as a person. Myself and several other JETs have already been through most of the problems you could encounter during your time as a JET. All you have to do is read on and you'll be one step closer to solving a problem and returning to what's most important, making a difference to your students in an out of the classroom.

Chapter 4: 64 Nuggets of Advice

For this section of the book I have listed problems that myself and several other JETs have faced and provided solutions. Some of these solutions are detailed while others might just be a short suggestion. In some problems a personal story is included as well, explaining how I resolved the issue and what I learned from it or how perhaps how I could've resolved it better. As I edit this book over the years I hope to include more problems and solutions so other JETs can learn from their predecessors and thrive in a foreign work environment. Without further delay, let's begin!

Section 1: Classroom Management and Dealing with Students

Your main role and place in the school is the classroom, so let's start there. Before we dive into the various scenarios, let's talk about the kind of teaching and atmosphere the JET Program wants their JETs to achieve. This is a classroom shared and taught as a team between a Japanese teacher of English and a native English speaker, also known as team-teaching. What is team-teaching? Team-teaching involves a balance where you the JET and the JTE share equal responsibility and support each other throughout the lesson. It is not a one-man show, it is a symbiotic relationship where you both teach and do relatively the same amount of work and contribute to the lesson and the education of your students.

Your school allows you to team-teach with other faculty members a certain number of classes each week and you get to make lessons that have a chance to enrich the lives of children. This is the ideal scenario where you get to work with teachers and contribute to their mission, you get teaching experience in the process, and you lower the amount of work for the JTE. It's a win-win-win scenario. You win, the teacher wins, and the students get to listen to a native speaker and emulate them. The program is a success! Right? Not all the time.

This is a section I'm sure some of you will find useful. I will be speaking from an extreme perspective here since there were times I had to use unorthodox methods due to the nature of my students and my school's culture. Hopefully you will never have to use any of these methods, but I never once failed using these. My school while improving its culture and image, was given a student score of around 30. This student score is referred to as *hensachi* (translated directly as standard deviation). In this system as of 2017 the highest *hensachi* is 80 and the lowest is 30. The *hensachi* is based off of the standardized test scores students are evaluated on to see if they can enter a school. Any score around a 30 and most Japanese folks will say "Ha! That means they can't even write their own name on a test without making a mistake." Harsh words, but this is the belief from several people I spoke with from teachers and parents, to total strangers. As you can imagine, I had a rowdy group of students that became more difficult as they got older and began to understand the system.

What is this system you might ask? Well it's the following. **Teachers cannot dismiss a student from class due to disruptive behavior as stated in the Japanese constitution guaranteeing that all students have a right to an education.** For more info and a good read check out this article: (https://www.japantimes.co.jp/community/2010/08/31/voices/discipline-in-schools-is-not-a-bad-thing/#.Wfb1vGhSyUk).

If you throw a student out of the classroom and you get parents calling the school complaining a foreign instructor is preventing their student from learning, you're done. Game over! While I agree this is unfair, remember this is not your home country. In Japan different expectations and rules are followed and protected.

If you see students falling asleep in classes and talking while a teacher is giving a lecture, there is really nothing you can do about it instantly and achieve permanent results. The students know the game and know the rules of the education system. I'm going to give you some instances and solutions and this is what myself and several other JETs experienced. Make sure you have a comfort level with your JTE before attempting anything. While the JTE is in charge of discipline, there may be times they will be reluctant to speak out and silence the students due to fear, or lack of confidence. This is where you will need to step up and take a different approach to the issue at hand. I will go down the list beginning with simple solutions and if the students are incredibly rude and refuse to listen, you will need to take drastic measures. While some of these behaviors are considered reasonable enough to throw a student out, you can't do that in

Japan and since the students know how to work the system, some might argue Japanese students are some of the most disrespectful you will encounter. But don't fall for this negative stereotype. These students just need a hand to guide them to adulthood.

Problem #1: 40 students are busy talking away and continuing to do so after the chime rings. They are ignoring the JTE's message to stand up and bow.

    Solution 1: In Japanese, tell the students yourself to stand up and listen to the JTE's instructions. This should grab their attention since they will be amazed you can speak Japanese and disrupting the flow of conversation. By focusing the classroom's attention on you, this will make the students more likely to stand up. The words for stand up and bow are 起立 *kiritsu*、礼 *rei*. Note that *rei* directly translates to the word "respect", though in the classroom setting it means "bow".

    Solution 2: Turn the lights off. This is not normal for a teacher to do. The students will wonder if they are going to watch a movie and will likely ask the teacher. Now that you have their attention, you can ask them to standup and they will likely obey. Now you can turn the lights back on.

    Solution 3: Say in a very big voice, "YO YO YO YO YO LISTEN UP PLEASE!" I mean SHOUT IT! You're competing against an army of 40 voices so you better be ready to out match them. The students will think you're a lunatic, but it will work and realize it's time to start the lesson. This was my most common tactic that would get the students to listen to me in large classes. It also put a smile on their face.

    Solution 4: Get a buzzer or airhorn (yes, an airhorn if necessary but warn the JTE ahead of time) of sorts and play it if the students don't listen. This goes against all protocol and anything a JTE will have gone through in their training, but when the students themselves are being rude, you can apply any tactic you wish so long as it doesn't physically harm a student or remove them from the classroom.

Problem #2: A few students are sleeping during an activity or lesson.

    Solution 1: Leave them alone. This is the usual method JTEs use especially if it is a rowdy student who is asleep. If this is the case, just let sleeping dogs lie and keep teaching the rest of the class.

    Solution 2: Call on them in class to answer a question. You'll embarrass them slightly, but it'll get them awake.

    Solution 3: Bump their desk and get them awake. *Do not physically touch them, especially if the person is the opposite sex*. A teacher can always argue they were just pacing the room and happened to bump their desk by accident.

    Solution 4: NOTE: <u>ONLY USE THIS TACTIC IF YOU AND THE JTE HAVE A VERY GOOD COMFORT LEVEL</u>

    Confiscate something of value from their desk and make a show of it. I did this method in my final two weeks of classes and it really worked wonders. Without touching any part of their body, from the top of their desk, confiscate a cell phone, a pencil case, or a book or bag or something of value the student will miss for sure when they wake up. You can confiscate something from the top of their desk, **if it's within easy reach**, but no taking wallets. Nothing containing money or IDs. Then once they wake up, you say "Tanaka are these yours?" The students will likely giggle and the sleepy student will be dumbfounded that you managed to take something from them right under their noses. Then tell them to come recollect their possessions and warn the class politely that you will take anything from sleeping students. Keep a tally of what you take and whether or not it is the 2nd or 3rd time you confiscate something. 2nd time = student must suffer 1 hour after class without the item. 3rd time = You get to keep the item for the entire day. 4th time = a phone call to the parents and possibly a meeting.

    If a parent argues it is rude to steal from their darling child, you politely tell them that sleeping in your class is the equivalent of saying "I don't exist. They don't believe what I say has any value. If they're sleeping in my class, they are also saying that they don't exist, which means their material possessions are available for grabs. Pay attention and stop sleeping in class, and we won't have any problems. Because believe me, if your son or daughter wants a job after high school and college, they can't be sleeping on the job. Consider it a life lesson." Believe me…<u>you will win this argument</u>. The parent might accuse you of sexual harassment, but guess what…<u>you didn't touch their body</u>. You're off the hook!

Problem #3: Students are talking in the back during your lesson or if they are ballzy, directly in front of you while sitting in the front row.

Solution 1: Tell them to please be quiet and then continue the lesson. This is a standard thing JTEs do so it's best to let them do it.

Solution 2: Remain quiet and just stare at them. The students will hopefully get the message and be quiet. It puts them on the spot.

Solution 3: Have them teach a section for the course. This is a standard trick JETs use because often times a lot of students who are disruptive merely just want attention due to problems back at home or negligent parents. The students might even do well and if not, they'll be reluctant to speak again. Or better yet, you can take this time to correct them and provide a good learning experience.

Solution 4: Have one of the students stand up and face the wall in the back of the classroom. This will make sure they don't have anyone to talk to.

Problem #4: Students testing you on the verge of sexual harassment

Here's another extreme scenario which I hope you will never have to face. In class the way we begin each lesson is the teachers enter, the teacher or class representative says class is starting and for everyone to "rise and bow", at which point class begins. Here's what happened, I was in the class with a JTE who I didn't exactly get along with towards the end of my time as a JET and I was doing my best to leave a good impression on him during my last year. Everything was going according to plan until a student at the very far back would lift up her skirt and flash me her underwear when the students would bow and salute me. The only people who saw her do this were two students in the back and myself. My JTE partner had his back turned and was writing on the board, so unfortunately, he did not see what happened. That student was clever and I'll give her credit for that, but I was dumbfounded on what to do.

Solution: I could've attempted to report it, but it would've been my word against hers, and I noticed her friends sitting next to her were snickering so they would no doubt side with her if it came to an argument. I realized it would be a male teacher arguing against a female student accusing her of harassment. Add into the equation that I'm a foreigner and that my JTE and I don't get along and you could probably guess like I did that any attempt at arguing against the student would clearly lead to a bad scenario that would likely make me the loser in this outcome. The worst case being that it could potentially risk my job and tarnish the JET program. It was in those four seconds of staring at her while she gave me a challenging look that I decided to ignore it and never bring up the issue to anyone. Being the cunning student that she was, she did it a few more times when my JTE's back was turned. Despite being shocked at first, I kept ignoring her and after a month, she finally gave up.

My advice to you when you come across sticky situations is to choose your battles wisely based on how you stand with the JTEs and your students. This occurred during our first month as a new class so they were testing me to see if they could get a rise and perhaps cause some drama. There are some battles worth fighting over and some that you should just ignore because they are not worth your time or perhaps too risky.

Problem #5: A fight breaks out in your class or you've walked into one.

Solution 1: Call the JTE over or another teacher. Students are sometimes sneaky in that most of the time they will ensure no teachers are around before a fight begins. They will also be less likely to treat you with respect until you earn it, so they won't consider you a real teacher at first. The JTE is in charge of discipline and not the JET, but sometimes the JTE lacks the confidence, power, or physical strength to break up a fight. In which case...

Solution 2: Put yourself in between the two students and shield the most injured student. You want to isolate the injured student away from the other student and get students to help you if possible. Eventually the commotion should bring a JTE or another teacher into the mix. NO MATTER WHAT HAPPENS: REMEMBER TO **NEVER EVER STRIKE A STUDENT**. THAT IS AN OFFENSE NO JET CAN ESCAPE. The student will also get in trouble for potentially striking a JET, so you will have the advantage when it comes to reporting.

Solution 3: (Only if you have the physical strength to pull this off) **Lift** (**NOT STRIKE**) both students off the ground and drop them in their chairs and yell "NO!" One JET I had the honor of working with at the post development conference told us how he once had to use physical force to set the tone for his class. And he's a big guy mind you, but also a gentle giant. While he was preparing his class, he witnessed two students fighting with no JTE in sight, and was forced to step in when it came to blows and blood was drawn. He picked up both students by the back of their collars and slammed them in their desks. The students were stunned at the strength of the JTE and realized fighting was not going to be an option to solving their problems in the classroom. From that day forward all students were timid and watched themselves around the JET. The power dynamic had shifted instantly and my friend used it to his advantage to gather their attention in class and further their English education despite teaching students at a technical high school where English isn't highly valued. As you can guess, he never had to use physical force again and the students respected him and paid attention in class.

Problem #6: You find an injured student

I remember one time on my way to class I discovered an injured 3rd-year student who was bleeding from his head. The boy foolishly tried to do a headstand and hit his head on a step at a bad angle causing blood to flow. I could've shouted "help! help!" but that would've likely caused panic right as classes had already started.

Solution 1: If you know where the nurse's office is, take the student there directly and do your best to explain the situation. In the event the nurse is not present, bring the injured student to the faculty room and let the teachers who aren't teaching that period tend to the student. Your JTE will understand you were looking out for a student if you're late to class. You'll also have witnesses who can vouch for you if the JTE attempts to criticize your actions.

Solution 2: What I did was grab the attention of a nearby student and explain the scenario using Japanese (be sure to use gestures or any means necessary if you can't speak it) to tell the student to stay with the injured student. Next, I asked the injured student who their homeroom teacher is and to point in the direction. Thankfully I knew the name of the boy's homeroom teacher when he told me, but if you don't know, interrupt the nearest teacher's classroom and calmly say "*mōshiwake gozaimasen. ..... sensei. Chotto ii desu ka.*" 申し訳ございません。。。先生。ちょっといいです か。 Bring the homeroom teacher or the nearby teacher to the injured student and they will take care of him or her. They will then excuse the student who stayed with the student and pardon them if they're late to class.

The goal here is to take care of the injured student as quickly as possible, bring a teacher who knows the location of the nurse's office, and get the student to safety. Being discreet will help the student avoid embarrassment instead of everyone jumping out into the hallway to see what the JET is panicking about. Stay calm and the situation will be taken care of and then you can get to class.

Problem #7: Dealing with bullies and their behavior towards another student

You'll have a couple of options when it comes to dealing with bullies in the classroom. The majority of bullying cases at my school were more verbal than physical and involved calling a student "faggot, gay, queer, or loser." I didn't understand these words in Japanese until the JTE pointed them out to me and I started studying more slang during my time as a JET. When I finally understood what was going on between one of my basketball students and another student, I had to act quickly and tell the student that what he was doing was wrong.

While I did say the JTE is in charge of discipline, sometimes they will look past or ignore bullying. In that event it may be up to you should you choose to rise to the occasion and discipline the bully. What you are able to accomplish will also depend on whether or not you can speak the language and make coherent sentences. In the event that you are able to speak Japanese, you can chew the student out privately and yell at them - which is what students are used to in Japan. You can try to have a private sit-down between the bully, the bullied and you and attempt to work out their differences, or get a JTE involved and deal with the problem as a group of four. **What you don't want to do is call out the bully and the bullied and yell at the bully in front of the entire class.** This will put the bully in a very uncomfortable position and they will face humiliation in class. As a general rule you never really want to put a student on the spot for wrong doing otherwise they will be afraid to speak up in class and could take out future anger on you.

My story: I remember when one of my basketball students was constantly pestering a boy name Shuh in my class. It wasn't until I knew what was going on that the incident was beginning to get out of hand. While my JTE could've handled the situation, she decided to let me address it since the bully was part of the basketball team and she felt I would have a better connection with him. After homeroom, I walked to the room to politely and quietly grab the bully's attention so I could talk to him privately. When I walked in the homeroom as it was finishing, I witnessed the bully pestering Shuh again physically and the homeroom teacher ignoring it. That's when I did a complete 180 and yelled at the bully to stop and to come with me. The class was silent. I almost never raise my voice. The bully and I stepped outside onto an outdoor hallway where I basically yelled at him.

Me: Sugiyama what in the hell are you doing? That's the third time today I saw you bullying Shuh. Is there a problem between you two?

Sugiyama: No...

Me: It sure looks like it to me because he keeps asking you to stop and you're not listening. On top of that I find you bullying him and wrestling him not only in my class, but in homeroom so I think something is up. I mean do you enjoy bullying him?

Sugiyama: Yes...I mean no. It's just that he's weird.

Me: I don't care what you think of him. Do you think I want to be doing this right now? Because I sure as hell don't. Ms. Takahashi told me to address the issue because we're in the same basketball team and if I don't settle this, I get in trouble. Do you want me to get in trouble?

Sugiyama: No of course I don't want you to get in trouble.

Me: Good because I like working with you in basketball and I don't want that to stop all of a sudden. Are you sorry for what've you done?

Sugiyama: Yes, (while avoiding my gaze).

Me: I don't believe you. So here's what is going to happen, you, me, and Shuh are going to talk outside here and settle this once and for all. Okay?

I gathered Shuh, and Sugiyama outside to discuss the issue privately, and Sugiyama ended up apologizing to Shuh. After that day the bullying stopped in my classes, but for all I know it could've continued in other locations. At the very least, the two behaved in my class, so I considered that a win.

To end this, how you handle bullying is going to depend on your conversation level, your relationship with the students and JTE in question, how long you've been at the school, and how confident and capable the homeroom teacher is when it comes to discipline. While you can't be the enforcer everywhere, if you can at least stop the bullying in your classroom, that's a victory.

Section 2: Teaching Scenarios

This part of the advice section addresses some of the more common complaints when it comes to team-teaching and also dealing with a JTE in class.

Problem #8: My JTE only gives me 10 minutes to teach in the classroom. What do I do?

Solution: This is not necessarily a bad thing. While you may feel insulted at first that you only get 10 minutes to teach, think of it as a warmup or preparation for you to run the classroom. Focus on making the 10 minutes useful for the students and bonus points to you if you can incorporate conversation practice.

Since you will likely have limited time to teach during your first few lessons, focus on one activity that is short, simple, and easy to do. It could be a worksheet with dialogue or maybe a mini quiz game where students can break their desks up. Personally, I'd start with an interactive worksheet and slowly introduce more complex activities once you earn the trust of the JTE and students.

Problem #9: My JTE is only using me as a human tape recorder where I read passages from a book and the students repeat after me.

Solution: Don't get discouraged. Think about it, the students get a chance to listen to native English and emulate it. The JTE probably doesn't know how to use a JET since they're not used to team-teaching. Go with the flow at first, and then slowly suggest something you can do with the students that will contribute to the target lesson. If you want to give the students more practice, read the sentence once, say it with them, then make them say the sentence or fragment by themselves. You could also suggest a quick-mini game or exercise or a worksheet for 10 or 15 minutes. (Notice how I'm referring to the previous solution) But the main point you should try to emphasize when proposing things is more exposure to native English and more speaking practice and less work for the teacher. Believe me, teachers love it when you take some of the workload and responsibility off of their shoulders. If for whatever reason the JTE is skeptical of your lesson idea, try it out on students in your English club if you have one. Once you prove it works, show it again and adjust it for a larger class size of 30 to 40 students.

Problem #10: You and the JTE keep interrupting each other in class.

Solution: Back when I was first getting used to working with new teachers in the semester, we didn't really have a flow or know how each would react. As a result, often times I would interrupt the JTE when I thought they were done talking or vice versa. If you interrupt each other by accident in the first lesson or two, carry on and don't worry about it. This should be a quick and easy solution you can fix after class by preparing a lesson plan and sitting down with the teacher.

This doesn't mean writing out a script, but it will mean that you need to write out the flow and structure of the lesson. If you look at the lesson plan I've attached to this E-book (*see table of contents*) you'll notice I have a designated time slot, and I list the roles of the JTE and JET. As long as you two stick to that plan, or whatever version of a lesson plan you create, you should minimize if not stop completely the amount of times you interrupt each other.

Problem #11: JTE asks you to suddenly prepare a lesson 10 minutes before class

Uh oh. Clearly there was some kind of miscommunication. Either the JTE expected you to have lessons prepared in advance, or maybe you misunderstood their intentions in an earlier meeting. Either way, you've got 10 minutes to make a lesson and quick. I will give you a quick panic room lesson and then we'll talk about how you can address the problem after class.

Quick lesson and Solution:

- **Opening 5 minutes**: Greet the class, ask a few students "how are you" while you walk around. Get them to say something besides the typical "I'm fine. Thanks. And you?"

- **10-15 minutes**: Breakup the class into teams by rows or in a group equivalent to number of spaces available to write on a chalk board. You're going to have a spelling race. One student from each group will come up to the board and at the same time race to spell a word. To make it a challenge you could ask them to spell the past tense or passive voice of a verb on the board. You say "eat", they have to spell "ate" and "eaten". The JTE keeps score and also helps judge and explains mistakes when necessary.

- **15 minutes**: Give the students a quick skit prompt. Tell them to use the grammar from their books and write a skit between 3-4 people on giving advice, persuasion, or asking how their weekend was.

- **20 minutes**: call the groups up one at a time to act out their skit in front of the class.

- **Remaining 2 minutes**: thank the groups for their participation and that you'll see them next time.

Now that you've survived that class, you need to sit down with your JTE and figure out why this happened. Make a plan to avoid this in the future. Perhaps set a schedule or routine where you have to meet each other two days before each class to go over the lesson plan and make adjustments. While this will vary depending on the flexibility of the JTE's schedule, try to set up a mutual agreement to avoid another repeat scenario.

Problem #12: JTE makes me teach by myself while they do nothing

While this scenario may appeal to you if you have a lot of confidence in your teaching abilities, in reality…this is not how the JET program is supposed to work. There are several things wrong with this picture. First, I hope you're not the only instructor in the room because you are legally not allowed to be left teaching a class by yourself. You also most likely don't have the license of a qualified teacher in Japan (Japan and the US have different standards, rules and ideologies when it comes to teaching). The biggest issue is if anything were to happen to a student such as a fight or a serious injury, the school and the JET Program will take a huge hit politically if you're the only teacher present. This problem also goes against the idea of the JET Program's new approach towards team-teaching and sharing the class. Finally, this promotes teachers to take advantage of the JET and dump their work on them which happened to me in my final semester.

I understand the JTEs are overworked, but dumping an entire class worth of preparation on the JET not only prevents you from preparing and helping other teachers, it will also increase the chances of failure since you don't know these students as well as the JTE and if something happens, you are forced to take the entire blame. In the event this happens, tell your supervisor what is going on and how you politely and respectfully recommend team-teaching so you can work with everyone rather than just make everyone's lessons for them. It doesn't matter if it's an entire lesson for each teacher one day a week, if you're preparing a new lesson to cater to each of the 11 classes or even 20 classes, you're going to get overworked and end up staying later and later in the day.

Remember that mistakes you make in the classroom can impact your relationships in the office, and those relationships will be brought back into the classroom, which will negatively impact your students' learning. And believe me, several awful days in the office can take a toll on you spiritually outside of the office. When I tried to get the JTEs involved in the lessons, a few of them were lazy and refused to meet with me saying I should be able to plan it by myself and grow up as a teacher. I understand the growing up part, but not when the JET is meant to be an ASSISTANT LANGUAGE TEACHER who ASSISTS not run the entire class.

Problem #13: JTE doesn't use me and I'm left alone at my desk

The JTE doesn't use you at all and you're left at your desk. This is one of the most common scenarios JETs face when they first enter the school. I completely understand the frustration one would feel if they recently obtained a degree in teaching. You're hoping to get experience abroad only to be met with disappointment when the JTEs don't utilize you, and force you to sit at your desk the entire day. Talk about a punch to the gut. But do not fret. You may feel as though you're at rock bottom, but rest assured it can't get any worse. The school cannot send you back home, and they're not doing this out of a personal vendetta against foreigners. What happens now though depends entirely upon you and your ability to rise out of this situation. Here's what I want you to do. Smile, be optimistic, and don't just sit on your butt all day.

Solutions: First, have a chat with your JTE and ask politely to observe the class from the back. Do not engage with any students. You're strictly there for observation. Take notes and try to think of a way you can help this teacher. Maybe it's a handout you could try to make or a study guide for the students or warmup activity. Remember, you're not at the level where you can team-teach with this instructor and you're currently viewed as an outsider looking in. You have to level up your relationship with the JTE bit by bit.

Once you've observed the teacher's class, sit down with the teacher again (bring your supervisor to translate if necessary) and compliment his or her class. No criticisms. You're not in any league to pass judgment on the instructor's class (especially if you're new to the whole formal teaching gig like I was). Keep the conversation on them and the students. Ask the teacher these questions. 1. What is their goal for the class this semester / year? 2. What do they wish they could do more in the class / what do they want to do, but feel they don't have time for? 3. What can you do to help them reach their goals and how can you support them? Ask, for example, if they want you to make some documents or a handout in preparation for a class. Do they want you to grade papers and correct English grammar? Do they want you to proofread documents they make? Would they like you to provide some extra practice for students who need help afterschool?

Notice, that the focus of this conversation is not "You have to use me! I feel like a victim." But rather, "What can I do to help your mission and goals for the class and take some of the work and pressure off of you?" If you keep the focus on the instructor and their goals, you will have a better chance for success.

If you don't know any Japanese or if you feel uncomfortable talking to one of the teachers, bring your supervisor or someone who can help translate your desire to help. The most important thing you're doing is taking action and trying to work with everyone. If the instructor for whatever reasons scratches their head and doesn't know what to do, that's okay. In that case, try to talk to students afterschool or between classes and do your best to get them to practice English. Bonus points if you can use the grammar they learn in each lesson.

Worst possibility for this scenario is, none of the teachers really know how to use you and you're left to your own devices. That's okay. Work on making some worksheets that complement the lessons in the textbooks and take on side projects. Get involved in extracurricular activities and if you're absolutely dying for teaching experience, volunteer to teach for free at some local events that are looking for volunteer instructors. There are other teaching jobs out there, but legally, you shouldn't be taking any additional paid jobs, and I will dive into that towards the end of the book.

In summary: First off never take the decision of a JTE to not utilize you in the classroom personally or as an attack against your race or country. Although the JET program is a well-known program, most of the schools in the country are finally just signing on to the program due to the Prime Minister's goal of having a native English speaker in every classroom by the

2020 Olympics. As a result, most JTEs as of when I'm writing this book, do not know how to use a JET in the classroom. Due to the lack of team-teaching experience and lack of handling foreigners in general, JTEs don't know the role of a JET and so they will likely feel awkward about it and won't say anything. Your job, if you encounter this situation, is to sit down one-on-one with each of your JTEs and ask them: what are their goals for the semester? What is the greatest challenge for their students (discipline, learning, etc.)? How they think they could use you to accomplish their goals? If after hearing them out, you come up with another idea, let them know right then and there.

Problem #14: The JTE will only allow you to read passages from the textbook, so you begin to find your work very dull and unfulfilling.

How this affected me: In the beginning it was a slight problem, but I learned to cope with it and it eventually changed thanks to one of the JTEs I worked with. After seeing me read to the students and how little experience they were getting just by repeating after me, a JTE I worked with came up with a new reading system for classrooms.

The goal was to provide each student one or two minutes of individual reading practice with me during certain classes. In our reading activities, students were given a certain paragraph to read a few days before the lesson. The JTE worked with the class for about five minutes the day before on pronunciation as a group. Students took notes on what they missed and were expected to practice at home. The day the JET came in, students warmed up by first listening to the JET read the passage from start to finish. Then the JET had the students repeat each paragraph and recite out loud. Once finished, the students sat with me one at a time and read the passage out loud within a time limit. The JET (myself) corrected the students on their pronunciation while they read and recommended certain changes. This repeats over several lessons and then the instructor graded them on their reading ability through a test at the end of the semester covering the same paragraph.

What you can do: While this is a bit of a detailed exercise, you could give it a shot and suggest it to the JTE if their students are having a lot of difficulty with reading comprehension and pronunciation. If they still refuse and only want you to read from the book, it's their loss, but on the bright side it means less work for you and you can focus on making worksheets and talking with students in the hallways. The key here is to look for the silver lining in any obstacle you encounter.

Problem #15: My JTE is absent! SOS

Personal Story: I was trying to be the best JET I could be by helping all of my teachers. One day my favorite teacher called the office 20 minutes before homeroom began to warn me that she had to rush her child to the hospital. Everyone was understanding, but the problem was there being no substitute capable of leading an English class and it was a first period class the day before midterm exam week. In my desire to help my school and make a difference, I took up the challenge and led the class. To my relief another English teacher came in early and was able to watch me to ensure that no student attempted to rebel or cause problems. To my surprise though, rather than the chaotic classroom I was expecting, everyone was quiet and nervous. I mean think about it, a foreign instructor who only knows a bit of the language and who doesn't have a license is teaching the class the day before the midterm exam...I think the thought on everyone's mind was "May the Gods help us!"

In the end we all had fun and completed the quiz game activity without a hitch. The English teacher who watched me complimented my classroom management skills without the help of a JTE and said, "Interesting. You can actually manage a class by yourself without any guidance or help from us. This is good and useful to know. Good work Adam!" Like any person wanting respect and to fit in the workplace, I was really pleased with the compliment, but I didn't realize that this was the beginning of what would lead to the end of my time as a JET.

Solution: If you have a lesson plan already in mind and you worked it out with the teacher. Try to teach it to the best of your ability only using English. I had an advantage since I could speak Japanese and could explain the rules to my students. In the event you had little to no communication with the JTE prior to the lesson, you could try to teach something by yourself, but it might be best to let the students have a study hall instead. It is always good to take opportunities to prove yourself in the classroom, but make sure you feel comfortable and ready to teach a specific lesson relevant to the curriculum if you suddenly have to teach alone.

Section 3: Student Behavioral Problems

Problem #16: Students are disrespectful in the hallways and always break rules.

Solution: Discipline was a common issue at my school due to the maturity level of my students. They would run and play tag in the hallways, jump through windows, slide down railings, and try to climb through the small windows above the classroom doors, which if done improperly, could lead to a broken limb or neck. I even had a group of six students, blind, bind and gag another student using his necktie as rope and parade him around the hallway.

What did I do to solve this? I played the game. What is this game you might ask? It's understanding your position in the food chain amongst your students and what you can and cannot get away with. For example, you can pull a student away to avoid and prevent a fight and you can also yell at them. However, you cannot physically touch them nor can they assault you. You're in a peculiar position since you're technically a guest and if any student attempted to attack you, they would be undoubtedly suspended and most likely expelled for not only attacking a teacher, but attacking a foreign representative and guest. My students also knew this so they dared not raise a hand towards me.

I used this to my advantage and developed stages. These were stages in which I would handle a problem. For example, I was known as a kind teacher who would almost never yell at his students. During my 1.8 years as a JET, I only raised my voice six times (Yes, I counted). The rest of the time I would slowly build up to it so my students knew not to continue their disruptive behavior. For example, when I caught my students running, I first told them politely to stop, if they ignored me I'd wait to catch them again and call out one of their names (it helps if you memorize their names). If you just yell "Stop running in the halls" you're just doing what the average teacher does and the students don't register that you're calling them out. But if you say their name and tell them to stop they might listen. The third time I caught them running, I stood in front of them and blocked the path of the lead boy, pulled him aside and said, "I don't want to yell at you. But if you don't stop you are going to get in trouble." It helped that I could speak Japanese, but if you can't, try to get one of them to follow you back to the office. If not, bring a teacher.

When I came across the bound and gagged student, I was thankfully with another Japanese teacher (not a JTE). We unbound the student and tried to explain politely to the students why their behavior was inappropriate. The five third-year students who did this ignored the Japanese teacher's explanation and turned their backs to her, and that's when I got mad. In English I shouted "Hey! Listen!" Both are easy words any student should understand. I then proceeded to scold them in Japanese and warned them to show more respect to their teacher and that what they did was dangerous and that they were ordered to return to their classroom. Any normal student would listen and politely return, but these students merely laughed and said "whatever man". That was their undoing.

If they ignore you and you have another teacher as a witness, you have everything you need to lambast them nine ways to Sunday. Bring the report to their homeroom teacher who has the power and authority to fully discipline them. After I explained what happened to their homeroom teacher, he kept them all afterschool, scolded them, called their parents, had them clean the classroom and forced them to apologize to me and the other teacher.

To be honest depending on the quality and moral fiber of your students, you may experience difficulty when it comes to disciplining them and telling them to stop destructive behavior. But if you report it to their homeroom teacher, that should delay if not prevent further problems.

Problem #17: Students harass or insult you in Japanese in and outside the classroom

Solution: I faced this on day one of my job where students had the nerve to talk about me as if I didn't know the language. I remember hearing things like "This guy is probably a virgin." "Klutz." "Loser." "Foreigner." "Wannabe Japanese" and other things such as "I bet he's well-endowed like other foreign males on television" etc. I'll be honest in saying this is not a normal situation, and I was placed in a rather hostile environment. The majority of these comments came at me because people assumed I didn't know the language. Let's face it, most of the students you'll be teaching are still maturing and have yet to speak with a foreigner, so they're going to try and say things to look cool in front of their friends even if it is inappropriate.

You can feign ignorance and let it slide or if you want to stop it and dish something back to show you understood, speak some Japanese. You don't have to yell, just speak calmly and show they can't get away with their behavior. When a girl said "I bet he's well-endowed like other foreign males on television" I calmly replied, "Sorry dear, I'm already spoken for and what you just said is inappropriate for a student to say." All of her friends just laughed at the girl's ignorance and word got around quickly that I could speak Japanese. From that day forward, the insults to my face in Japanese stopped.

I realize that most JETs may not have the ability to speak Japanese and that even if you do, you may want to feign ignorance for the sake of providing an "English only environment" for your students. I admire and respect that resolve, but make sure your students aren't going to take advantage of you. If necessary, bring the topic up to your supervisor or teacher and have them address the issue to the students in question.

It's important to remember that you're dealing with adolescents who are still trying to navigate the world and have been given the additional challenge of speaking to a foreigner. They will say things thinking you don't understand, and your job in this situation is to teach them that it is rude to talk about someone present in a foreign language. If the issue is still getting out of hand, bring it up to a teacher. Don't get angry at them. If anything, try to talk to them in English and that should clam a few of them up since they don't want to look foolish in front of their friends.

Problem #18: Students pretending to not understand you in the classroom and outside it to avoid dealing with you.

Once my reputation for speaking Japanese spread, some students knew they couldn't get away with bad-mouthing me. They also didn't want to look foolish in front of their friends so when I tried to get their attention in class or outside in English and Japanese, they chose the easy way out and tried to ignore me.

Solution: Depending on what you're trying to convey to the student, you can let it slide or if it's something important, you can try the following in order:

1. Say their name while walking next to them.

2. At the end of class when you teach them, say "Mr. or Ms. ... I need to speak with you after class." The teacher should be able to translate. Or you can say "(name) san, sumimasen kurasu no ato, watashi to hanashite kudasai". _____さん、すみません。クラスの後、私と話してください。

3. Last resort is bringing the issue to their homeroom teacher which will then lead to a sit down where you and the student will talk to each other in front of the homeroom teacher.

Problem #19: Students do not behave well during club activities

This was not a common problem amongst JETs since most of the students were well behaved and the club coach was present, but you know students... they're smart. They know the system and always try to find loopholes. The challenge you face is leveling up your image so the students know they cannot get away with misbehavior. If you can speak Japanese, it makes things much easier, but if you have to communicate the problem to a JTE and then to a club supervisor, it increases the chances of miscommunication.

Most JETs will bounce from club activity to club activity and that's fine, but if you want to carry some weight in what you can say or do and manage students in a club, you need to stick with one. I remember when the basketball club was rampant with discipline problems due to the 2nd year students, and half the time they didn't listen. Over several months I had to build an image that showed they couldn't get away with snide comments and misbehaving. Here's an example of handling a situation while you're slowly trying to gain authority and respect within a club activity.

Personal Story: I had a young boy named Segawa who was a real troublemaker and he'd listen in class for the most part, but he knew my boundaries and would always push them. He understood that I left the discipline to the basketball coach and that I was mainly in charge of guaranteeing the boys exercised and actively participated in club activities.

Flash back to November. It was Thanksgiving afternoon, and although the Japanese don't celebrate it, I remember this being the most disgusting Thanksgiving ever thanks to Segawa. At this point in my JET journey, I'm the second assistant to the boys' basketball club and every Thursday we had to run three miles. We're stretching outside and no one is around. The basketball coach had a meeting so he left us to our own devices leaving me in charge. The boys are joking while stretching and that's when they began to talk about their private parts and who had the bigger package. Segawa decided to drop his pants and proclaim "Feast your eyes on my golden nuts." I was appalled that a student dared do that in front of me. I thought about yelling at him and forcing him to pull his pants up but I knew he would swing the story to say I was trying to sexually harass him.

Here's what I did. I rolled my eyes in annoyance and I said "OKAY! STRETCHING IS OVER WE'RE RUNNING." I stuck to the role the head coach gave me and began running. The boys were shocked that I started making them run halfway through stretching and Segawa was embarrassed because everyone had a head start and he often bragged about being the fastest. I warned Segawa not to do it again in private and normally I would've reported it to the head coach, but here is the problem and another reason why I knew I'd have difficulty finding anyone to believe me. You have 11 boys and one teacher. The teacher being the foreigner and the rest being friends and Japanese. Had I reported it, they would have easily construed my story saying that I did not understand what they were saying and that I was not seeing well. Think about it, 11 stories vs. one, and I had only been on the job for three months.

Solution: I slowly gained the ability to report similar incidents after being able to give speeches in Japanese at the basketball practices. After every practice the coach would point out the students' mistakes. He would hardly ever compliment them on their successes. Perhaps this made them grow, I'm not sure, but I learned that I could start gaining some authority if I chimed in. I waited for the assistant coach to speak, then I would speak. Eventually the boys began to respect my authority more and I won over the respect of the coach. Towards the end of the first year, when I told students to get back to practice, it helped that I not only participated with them, but also developed an image through the speeches at the end of practice.

Problem #20: Students asking inappropriate questions.

I had this happen to me a few times and I thankfully only dealt with a minor incident or two. Other JETs I've spoken with had a more serious encounter. I will touch upon both in this problem. My experiences with this scenario were more on the verbal side. It was my second year on the job and one of my students had grown comfortable with me. He called me the crazy teacher and I called him the wild boy due to his enthusiasm in my classes. Afterschool as I was talking with him and a few of his classmates about music, he asked me if I had a girlfriend. Wanting to be mysterious, I said "that's a secret." He then followed up with, "Are you experienced?" I didn't understand what he meant so I followed up on it. He then said in broken English, "Adam have sex before?" As you can guess, my mouth dropped a little at the question since it was in English. I knew I was only going to be around for a year or two, so I said jokingly I'd tell him after he graduated.

What I really should've done: This response satisfied his curiosity and others' who asked me different, but similar questions about English curse words and sexual content. As I reflect upon this though, my answer wasn't a very good one. The professional response would be to politely explain that sexual questions are not the type of question to ask your current teacher, but more towards your friends who are the same age group and even then, it is risky since that is a private matter. Because I didn't explain that rule, likely the next JET who took my place is going to experience a similar question, and I could've made it easier had I led the charge in explaining the boundaries you need to set when asking a sexual question towards a JET or foreigner.

This next story of inappropriate behavior belongs to another JET. This JET was at a high school and it was Sports Day. The student in question was pleased since he recently discovered he earned a great grade in his class thanks to the JET's help and wanted to thank him, while also taking a dare from his female classmates. The dare was likely to cop a feel on the JET's private area. The student surprised the JET in the hallway from behind and gave the JET a hug and at the same time placed his hand on the JET's private parts. The JET was shocked, and even more so when the student turned around to the girls and said "Yup! It's a big one!" in Japanese.

I'm glad I did not have to deal with this story, but I do feel bad for my fellow JET. He had every right to grab the student by the ear and scold him in the teacher's room, but he kept his cool. Instead of yelling at the student and causing a possible rift in their relationship, he calmly explained that his actions were inappropriate to JETs, foreigners, and anyone in general. The JET could speak fluent Japanese, so communication was not a problem, but if you lack the Japanese language skills, my recommendation is to take the student into the teacher's lounge and with the help of a translator, explain the concept of sexual harassment in a calm manner. It is easy in my opinion to get angry at some of the students, but as I explained earlier you are viewed as a second parent who is responsible for educating the children where the primary parent failed. If the same student does this again to you, then absolutely scold them and punish them according to the Japanese school system. But what I ask is that you take the role of a teacher first and then punisher later.

Problem #21: One of your students has a crush on you and is taking it too far.

I only had to deal with this problem once and was able to end it quickly. While I was volunteering at the middle school, I noticed that one of the students had several horizontal cuts along her wrist. Being the concerned teacher, I spoke with the student in private between classes. She mentioned that the marks were nothing and how she was upset over a boy who hurt her feelings a long time ago. Taking the mindset of a parental figure, I took her aside and explained that growing up is hard. Your mind is trying to process everything that is happening and it can be overwhelming. I told her to always be open to talking to her homeroom teacher and the school nurse if she ever needed someone to listen to her. Since I was not a licensed teacher and was only visiting the school once a month, I couldn't really make an impact. Before I left for the day, I brought it up to her homeroom teacher and the nurse to make sure she'd have people looking out for her. I was in for a bit of a shock when the nurse and homeroom teacher gave me concerning looks. Both teachers told me to watch out for her since she caused several problems with the school previously over boys. I thought to myself sarcastically, "Great! I try to do the right thing and it turns out it was not the best decision, but how was I supposed to know?" The answer was that I wasn't, and before I knew it, the problem was just beginning.

Before the day ended, the student passed me a quick note explaining how it was really touching that I was concerned over her injuries and that she never had a teacher like that. She said I made her day and that she was excited to speak with me again next time and that she promised to stop hurting herself. At least she would stop, but a part of me began to worry after hearing the teachers say "she is a trouble maker and has a history with boys."

Sure enough, my fears were justified when I visited their school festival. The female student grabbed my arm from behind and began to escort me down the hall as if we were prom dates. Within seconds I politely and gently removed my arm from her grip and explained how I was juggling food as an excuse. Thankfully she bought it and persisted that I let her show me around. In this kind of situation, I knew that my words could possibly have a negative impact on her, so I set definite and discreet boundaries by saying, "Sure! I'd love to see your school. It's just that I only have an hour to spare before I have to report back to my school." (This was a lie, but I did not want to be trapped by the student and be possibly accused of wrongdoing. At the same time though, I also did not want to be the catalyst for what could possibly cause the student to inflict further self-harm or even suicide). For the next hour I allowed the student to give me a tour of her school and introduce me to her brass band club. We did a little shopping at the craft fair, and at the end I thanked her and went home. No problems caused and I probably made her day by spending time with her. I only saw the student one more time in December for a Kite Flying event, but it was only in passing, so thankfully she did not have a chance to communicate with me for too long.

Solution: If you ever have a student who potentially shows any kind of romantic interest in you, be careful with how you handle it. Don't just simply ignore the student since you might cause some serious damage if the student suffers from depression or has a history of self-harm.

In the event the student writes you a love letter or is persistent in trying to spend time with you, or worse, follows you home, bring up the issue to your supervisor, the student's homeroom teacher, or another teacher you trust. Whatever you do, DO NOT try to settle the issue with the student by yourself. Lovestruck students can be unpredictable and might attempt to touch you. If another teacher walks in on what appears to be a teacher engaging in possible inappropriate conduct, you can kiss your job goodbye. If push comes to shove, schedule an appointment after school to talk to the student in the teacher's room in the presence of their homeroom teacher.

First ask the student politely why they're behaving the way they're behaving around you. See if they'll admit to their feelings or if it's perhaps one big misunderstanding. Then tell your side of the story and let the homeroom teacher educate the student on inappropriate behavior. At my school we had a lot of issues between students and teachers because the students didn't understand what was inappropriate between a student and a teacher and the boundaries that both sides needed to respect. If the situation becomes more than you can tolerate, involve a third party who is a teacher and talk it out.

Problem #22: My student is being abused at home

When I walked down to the vending machine during my lunch break one of my students walked in late to school. I jokingly chided him that he should stop playing video games... until I saw his face. The boy had bruises all along the right side and he even had a makeshift bandage on his cheek. He said it was nothing and that he fell. I let it slide at first, until two days later I saw additional bruises and asked the student privately as to what was going on. It turns out the student failed his midterm exams and so his mother beat him as punishment. Like any concerned teacher would do, I recommended the boy see the school guidance counselor for help, and he told me he already was. I was hoping as the bruises got worse the counselor would report the issue to child services and the boy and his family would be given proper counseling, but all the counselor did was give the boy tips on how to not anger his abusive parent. In the end, I spoke with the guidance counselor who admitted there was nothing he could do about it. I was angry and felt that the boy should be kept separated from the mother, but I couldn't voice that opinion. I'm a foreigner and am not a certified guidance counselor. But the sad truth is, the Japanese aren't very good at dealing with issues of domestic violence. It's one of those topics that is often swept under the rug since to have it discussed openly is viewed as embarrassing to all parties involved.

As a JET, your abilities to handle domestic violence are quite limited. If you see a student with injuries and they openly tell you it is domestic violence, you can report it to their homeroom teacher. If for whatever reason you believe the homeroom teacher won't act, take it up to the guidance counselor immediately. If the student wishes to talk to you for help and if they feel comfortable telling you about the problems at home, listen and offer minimal advice. Unless you're a former professional psychologist, you're likely not in a position to solve the student's problems directly. The best you can do is provide moral support for them and to be present when they need a shoulder to lean or cry on. The JET program's guidelines regarding the role of an ALT, CIR, and SEA are quite strict, and to go beyond those roles could put your job in jeopardy. This is the only problem as a JET where you will likely need outside help.

Problem #23: My student is involved in self-harm and has come to me for help

This is another problem I pray you don't have to deal with during your time as a JET. Depending on the situation, it can get ugly and if you provide the wrong advice, it could cost a life. These are the kind of situations JETs are not equipped to handle and sadly we come across these from time to time. When I was running the English club, I did my best to make it a safe space for all students. We were diverse with most of our crew consisting of foreign students who immigrated to Japan two or three years ago. One day, one of my most talented students came up to me and was in tears. We had yet to begin English club for the day and so I had time to chat. Ming showed me her wrists and said how difficult it was to find friends in her grade and how the only friends she had were in English club, so she felt frustrated. Apparently, Ming had been cutting her wrists to cope with depression and the feeling of not belonging to any core group of friends. That day I ensured she was having a fun time and I suggested she wear a sweater so the other students wouldn't feel put off by her injuries.

Next, I reported the incident to Ming's homeroom teacher since I knew she was the type who took her job seriously and cared for her students. Ming got the help she needed and was able to eventually make some friends in her homeroom in addition to English club thanks to the efforts of her homeroom teacher. When I encountered this problem, I really wish the JET Program provided some kind of training for this kind of scenario. Like I've said before, often times the most important responsibility is not English education, but rather cultural sharing and from time to time providing the safety and wellbeing of our students.

If you have a student suffering from depression whose life may be in danger,

Do:

- Listen to them
- Talk to them
- Tell their homeroom teacher and your supervisor to see if there is any standard procedure you need to carry out within your school's guidelines. (Every school has a different procedure).
- Check in on the student privately the next day and every once in a while.

Do Not:

- Tell other students
- Tell the student's parents (leave that to the homeroom teacher since that could wind you in trouble for breaking rank)
- Smother the student with attention
- Try to offer specialized counseling
- Take the student out to dinner

Problem #24: What to do with an upset student

My own story: While you're working in Japan, it is important to remember that the expectations and meanings of actions are viewed completely different than in your home country. Sometimes you doing the right thing can be viewed as frightening or improper, and it will cost you relationships if you're not careful. The story I'm about to tell you is a sad one. If you can learn from my mistake and keep on going, awesome.

110

I remember a student named Kasagawa. She always stood out because whenever she visited the teacher's room, she always made an effort to talk to me in broken English to make me feel welcome to her school. When I was still adjusting to my job, talking to her in English made me feel like a teacher and that I was doing something right. I appreciated it and seeing her bubbly attitude made every teacher's day a little brighter. Kasagawa was bright, energetic, and unfortunately had difficulty with her courses. One day I walked inside the teacher's room to see her crying in front of her homeroom teacher. It turns out her poor grades were going to possibly cost her graduation and her dream job of working as a waitress in a historical restaurant. Although I wasn't her homeroom teacher, I felt like I should do something to cheer her up and give back to all the times she reached out to me and made me feel welcome at the school. I took a little card and wrote her a good luck message since final exams were approaching. I told her the teachers were cheering her on and wanted her to succeed on her finals. I ended the message with study hard and get some sleep and give the exam her best shot and to have no regrets when she put down her pencil. The message I wrote was an empowering message similar to one I received during midterms from my mentor when I was a freshman in college. I appreciated it. Little did I know…Kasagawa would not.

After reading my message, Kasagawa misconstrued my intentions and believed the three-sentence note to be a love letter. That and she believed it was not my place to cheer her on because she viewed me as an outsider, and that I was not her homeroom teacher. I learned this from another student who told me about what happened. The good news was she passed her exams so I have a little hope that the message helped, but after finals she completely snubbed me. She would make snide comments towards me in the hallway and would make an effort to speak to every teacher but me when she visited the faculty room. I'll admit it hurt especially when teachers would ask… "Why is Kasagawa clearly ignoring you?" I explained my actions and they told me that she likely viewed my action as improper since I was not her homeroom teacher and that it was intrusive in her eyes.

The lesson learned: You can offer moral support vocally and provide an ear to the student, **but never put it in writing**. Letters, even

111

small ones, are viewed as serious and sacred to students in Japan. It is also a matter of rank since while you are a sensei in Japanese society, your rank in the eyes of students is likely below their homeroom teacher. Only lend help if the student comes directly to you seeking assistance, and even then, be careful.

Section 4: Office Culture

This next set of problems involves the type of scenarios you may possibly encounter in the office. These problems range from social issues, to timing, and cultural values. While I was at a troubled school that was known to have student discipline issues, I discovered that a lot of issues stemmed from the faculty room. As I reflect upon these issues and how I solved them, I can't help but wonder if perhaps these issues often spilled over and were at times the cause of some classroom problems I faced. My goal here is to help you identify and quickly resolve these problems so you can get back to teaching.

Problem #25: My train is late or delayed and I'm going to be late for class.

It happens to everyone, but at some point, your train will run late or worse the delay is going to cause you to be late for class. What should you do when you're late to the office? First, call your office immediately and if for some reason no one is there, email your supervisor or anyone you can get a hold of. Next take the fastest route to your school. Then I want you _**TO NOT**_ grab a slip of paper that the train conductors pass out and sign to people who need it to prove the train was late. Nowadays that information can be found online and if you wait in line for a pass, you'll likely be waiting with several dozen or close to 100 people depending on the accident or delay. That could easily eat up another 30-40 minutes of time and with you on the clock and your students waiting, it's not the best course of action. Open communication via phone and email and honesty is better, so keep your supervisor and those at your office in the loop and you'll be just fine. If they give you grief for not having the slip of paper, ask them "Would you rather I be late by an additional 30 minutes and miss class with my fellow teacher?" I promise you that will silence anyone who gives you grief. When a teacher began to attack me for not having the slip of paper, I told them my logic and the other teachers backed up my argument.

How to prevent this scenario and another course of action: After your first day of work, (especially if you are based in a large city) I recommend you take a train map and your cellphone with you to a coffee shop and plan out three routes you could take in the event your train was delayed or shutdown. Commit them to memory and hopefully you'll never have to use them. Next download this app: Y!norikaeannai Y!乗換案内 this app will allow you to see the schedule for all trains and subways in the area in addition to seeing which carts stop in front of the nearest exit or transition point to a different train line. This app has saved me several times when I've needed to navigate back home due to a freak accident from a storm or a person committing suicide by jumping in front of an oncoming train. Believe me, this happens. And if you're trying to beat a storm so you're not stranded in the open, knowing alternative routes to get back home can really help.

Outside shot of Ikebukuro station. A great shopping area where you'll always find something to check out.

Problem #26: The JTE keeps shutting down your lesson plan ideas

This problem is likely the most common issue JETs encountered during their stay. They'd make a lesson plan for their JTE, who would briefly look it over and say either "Sorry I can't use this." Or "This won't work."

Solution: It's easy to let the conversation die as soon as the JTE says this since they are busy and you don't want to disturb them. But if you want to get your lessons approved, it's up to you to keep that conversation going. First thing you want to do is actually tell the teacher ahead of time you'd like to meet with them and set up an appropriate time. The trick to this is to be ahead of your lessons and provide adequate time to not only let the JTE read your lesson, but provide enough time in the schedule to meet a 2nd time should they not like the lesson and want you to redo it. From my experience, I recommend a good three or four days.

Now assuming you've scheduled the meeting and the JTE has said the classic "I can't use this or it won't work" explanation, here's what you can say to lead to a productive meeting.

- "What would you fix in order to have this lesson be used?"
- "What is the lesson plan's main weakness?"
- "Can we perhaps combine one part of the lesson with something you have in mind?"
- "What is your idea for the lesson?"
- "If I wanted to make my lesson idea better and use it for a later date, what can we do differently?"

If the JTE for whatever reason is elusive and doesn't know how to respond to any of these questions, that's okay. Throw your own ideas out there in this meeting. The number one reason why JETs get their lessons blocked is because they meet perhaps one period before the class is scheduled to take place, and that is setting yourself up for disaster.

If you have a super stubborn JTE who just doesn't want to try anything new in their lesson, you can adjust to them. Visit their class and take notes on what they teach. Try to come up with an activity or game that is similar to what the JTE is already doing and that they'll have a comfort level with.

If the JTE continues to refuse your ideas, try out those ideas in other classes and prove they work. There was one particular game I wanted to try, but one of the JTEs was nervous about it because she had never done it before. However, the male JTE I worked with loved it so much that he was raving about how his students were jumping up and down for the first time in class eager to answer an English question. Once the skeptical JTE heard this, not only once but twice from a second JTE, she tried the lesson and liked it. From that day forward, I had an easier time getting my lessons approved by the strictest JTE.

In short if you want your lessons approved, provide adequate time to meet twice and adjust. Then follow up on the JTE's remarks and if you still have trouble getting lessons approved, try them out on other teachers or even try them out on your English Conversation club.

Problem #27: You're not allowed to participate in graduation or the entrance ceremony

Thankfully this was not an issue I had to experience, but I do know several JETs who weren't allowed to sit with the teachers or even watch the ceremony. Here are some story posts from various JETs on social media.

Story 1: I got into my black suit expecting to see my students graduate and was looking forward to the day's events. When I arrived at the teacher's room, my supervisor pulled me aside and apologized for I was not allowed to sit inside the auditorium for graduation. They sent me to the broadcasting room until it was over.

Story 2: I showed up to work and was surprised to see everyone dressed up. Apparently, graduation was today and no one told me about it. I was so upset and was later told I wouldn't be allowed to sit with the teachers, but could watch the ceremony as a visitor if I sat with the parents.

Solution: There are several theories as to why some JETs are not allowed to attend graduation, but if you want to increase your chances of attendance, know when the event is and mark it on your calendar. It's just like I mentioned on day one. This ties into everyone's expectations of you after the first three months. Since you're now in a professional work environment, don't expect the teachers to guide you by the hand for each event. All schools have an academic calendar they provide to the staff and there is no reason why you shouldn't be allowed to get one and keep track of events. If you stay on top of the events and know the school schedule, you'll be more likely given access to these events. If you're being responsible, school events should not take you by surprise.

月		2 月			3		
	1	月	学年末考査(3) 終 ↓		1	火	PTA
	2	火			2	水	
	3	水	修学旅行(2)始 ↑		3	木	学年末考 個別相談
	4	木			4	金	
	5	金	修学旅行(2) 終 ↓		5	土	
	6	土			6	日	
業日終	7	日			7	月	
○	8	月	成績報告 13:00(3)		8	火	学年末考 (1,2)終
明会③	9	火	学力調査		9	水	入選会場 [3h〜]
	10	水		○	10	木	入学者選抜 休業日
テスト	11	木	建国記念の日		11	金	入選採点 PTA運営委員
△	12	金	学校運営連絡 協議会		12	土	
	13	土	講習				

Sample Academic Calendar

RUMOR BASH: I've noticed many JETs blame the Board of Education for not being allowed to attend the graduation ceremony, but I'm going to smash that idea into the ground right now. If your vice principal says you cannot attend graduation because of a policy from the Board of Education, they are mistaken. I was allowed to see all of my students graduate and so did other JETs. Our JET leader even confirmed at our

Professional Development Training in front of several Board of Education members, that the BOE never made any such rule. This is either what I hope to be a misunderstanding on the vice principal's part because he is in charge of seating, or it's blatant racism. I also hope that maybe he just simply forgot to put your name down on the seating chart, but still... it's not like you couldn't just bring a chair with you. Yes, the teachers have assigned seats, but having an extra chair at the side and then bring it over and sit down in it afterwards should not be that big of a deal.

The vice principal plans out the seating chart two months in advance, so get your supervisor with you and ask to be seated. If you attend **YOU MUST STAND** for the Japanese National Anthem. To not stand at attention during their national anthem is a huge slap in the face to the country and an instructor was even punished for this. Not at my school, but a Japanese teacher was suspended for not standing at graduation during the Japanese National Anthem. Trust me, you don't want to be the next target on television. Suck up your pride and just lip sync if you feel self-conscious or unsure, but do not sit down when everyone starts singing. This story involving the punished teacher is one of the possible theories as to why some JETs can't participate in graduation due to the sensitive topic of the national anthem, but that remains to be determined. My vice principal pulled me aside the day of graduation and explained how important it was for me to sing the national anthem if I wanted to participate as a teacher.

Problem #28: You're being overworked.
This was the most serious problem I faced during my second year as a JET. From my experience this happens gradually due to two reasons. 1. The JET is eager to prove him or herself in the office and thus volunteers to take on additional work when they don't realize how much effort it takes. 2. The JTEs seeing this tremendous effort from the JET are pleased, but then they get too used to this work ethic from the JET and thus expect tremendous results to be the norm. By the end, the JET feels stuck because they want to ask for help, but they don't want to look bad in front of their co-workers.

How this impacted me: Remember how I mentioned my desire to help out in the school, so I volunteered to teach a class by myself? Well that action built me a reputation as becoming a reliable teacher who can teach solo. While this was great and the JTEs gave me more freedom in the classroom, it slowly started to snowball to the point where I couldn't manage anymore. Since every teacher was different, it required me to come up with several different activities that were similar, but also catered to the classrooms' needs. As soon as I was fine-tuning the current lessons for the next classes, I had to start the following week's lessons and think ahead as to how to make them all unique. All of this combined with inner departmental conflicts led to a lot of work being placed on me and having me teach 11 classes by myself each week using a different lesson. Towards the end of the semester, the work kept piling on and I had to stay at the school until 9:00 pm or even later and thus not arrive at my apartment until 10:30 pm or at one time 11:00 pm at night. Then I had wake up and be out the door for work by 6:30 am. This was not an ideal lifestyle and one I do not recommend to any JET.

On top of the increasing expectations to lead the classes, I was also given full responsibility for an English club. One of my JTE's came up to me and said "Let's start an English club together!" I was happy because this was also a part of my job and I thought I could get more responsibility since I was already doing well with the boys and girls basketball clubs. One more club shouldn't hurt especially if the JTE and I collaborate and team-teach.

Unfortunately, this was not the case. As soon as I sat down with the JTE to plan the first club meeting's activities, he said "Oh! Actually, I meant for you to take full responsibility with the English club and make the games and lessons. I'm too busy. Sorry. I am just here to sponsor the club and provide a signature." You can imagine how frustrated I was. Not only was I losing a day with the girls basketball team (which eventually led to it falling apart), but I also had an extra club's preparation worth of work. In the end I had an additional two hours' worth of content to plan on top of the normal lessons. It's one thing if you're doing private conversation lessons, but if it's a group activity, you have to come up with plans in advance and it would've been nice had the JTE been clear and honest with his intentions from the start.

What I should've done: I should've thrown away my stubborn pride, come clean, and spoken to my advisor or another JTE whom I trusted. I should've also spoken to the JET Facebook group for help, and if necessary speak with the vice principal. When I was a JET, I focused on my job, and trying to keep the peace with the other teachers. But that led to me taking on too many responsibilities and getting burned out. Back then the biggest fear I had was standing out in the workplace and causing problems. I didn't want to complain or make a big issue about anything because I was worried about the repercussions the Japanese faculty would have against me if I complained.

Whatever you do, do not simply take the work and do it for other teachers to make a point. When a faculty member is sick for a day that is totally understandable. You should do your best to help them out. But if a faculty member repeatedly refuses to help in the classroom, and slowly starts to take advantage of you, you have a problem.

To avoid being taken advantage of here are some tips. Never volunteer to take a position or opportunity to teach a class by yourself to prove a point. Stick to your role as an assistant language teacher and don't let any teachers give you responsibilities you don't feel comfortable with. I put up with the demand for my solo lessons for more than a year and when I learned that my family needed me back home and that my situation was only getting worse, I knew it was time to quit my job. I do not want any person to go through what I went through since mistakes you make in the classroom can impact your relationships in the office. Those issues will likely be brought back into the classroom, which will negatively impact your students' learning and the cycle feeds itself. Several awful days in the office can take a toll on you emotionally off hours. When I tried to get the JTEs involved in the lessons, some of them refused to meet with me saying I should be able to plan it by myself and grow up as a teacher. Believe me, the last four months of my time as a JET were not fun due to a few uncooperative employees.

Problem #29: Your Japanese co-worker asks you a sexual question or perhaps touches you inappropriately

For any problem involving sexual harassment regardless of whether you're male or female, you do not have to take it. While it would be normal for us to immediately report the problem to HR at work, we need to take a slightly different approach. If you feel uncomfortable due to a question or because someone is touching you, here's what I believe you should do. Tell the person right then and there immediately, politely, but firmly, to stop. Tell them that you feel very uncomfortable, and that in your home country, questions regarding sexual nature or one's body are viewed as inappropriate. Hopefully, the co-worker will stop and learn that they cannot ask you or any JET questions such as this without causing offense. I remember when some male and female co-workers questioned me about my racial preferences in the bedroom, how large my p***s was, and whether it was true American females had the biggest breasts in the world. I told them that those questions were inappropriate. They apologized and said they wouldn't ask a foreigner those questions ever again.

The reason why you're likely to get asked these questions regardless of your gender is because you're foreign. Remember, many Japanese people still don't have experience talking to people outside of Japan due to what I call "The Island Effect." They've been isolated from foreigners and other cultures their entire lives and so when they see someone different, their manners filter turns off and they feel as if they have permission to ask anything they want. I agree this attitude is quite ignorant, but this is the moment where you can do your job and educate them on how to treat foreigners with respect. Rather than report the teacher to HR, teach them how to interact with foreigners. If for some reason they do it again and persist in the awkward questions despite you telling them to stop and teaching them why it's bad, go immediately to HR and report them and then report the offensive behavior to the vice principal. At that point you show no mercy. I guarantee you that if the vice principal is any good at his job, he will chew out the teacher on the spot or in private. After taking the appropriate steps, you will not be bothered again. If the problem continues with the same co-worker, take the issue to someone at the Board of Education, and you can start developing a case to get the co-worker transferred instantly or better yet removed from their job permanently. I know this will work because that is what happened to one of my fellow JET's co-workers.

Problem #30: Not being invited to enkais or parties

This was also a very common problem amongst JETs in Tokyo. Teachers would go out and celebrate after a school event or even after a Friday and they wouldn't invite the JET. First, the problem is not you, it's them. I want you to repeat this to yourself, "It is not me. It is them." Most likely the reason why they didn't invite you was because they are worried you would feel bored since they're all speaking Japanese and you'll likely not be able to keep up with the pace. Another possible reason is they lack confidence in their English to speak with you so they'd be embarrassed if they made a mistake. It is not because they are racist. From my experience the Japanese are some of the kindest and most welcoming people, but they're often shy and have a lot of walls one must break before establishing trust.

 Solution: Take the initiative yourself and throw your own *enkai*. It doesn't matter if only one or two teachers show up, focus on having a good time. That's what I did and I invited teachers I knew wanted to develop a good working relationship and I did my best to speak Japanese the entire time. If you don't have confidence in your Japanese, then invite all of the English teachers instead. If you want to speak Japanese, invite half and half. Sometimes throwing a "Guys Night" or "Ladies Night" can be a great way to make some good connections in the office.

 HEADS UP: Under no circumstances are you allowed to invite a group of students out to dinner. When I was planning to invite students from the English club to a cheap restaurant to celebrate the end of the year I got several red flags. Even if you won the state championships, as you see in Japanese anime where the coach takes the students out to eat dinner after a tough match, that doesn't happen in real life. The teacher in this case would go home and let the students celebrate on their own. This is to maintain the relationship of respect between teacher and student. Once those barriers begin to come down, you may have a hard time winning the students' respect over in the classroom when it comes to disciplining them because instead of seeing you as an authority figure, they will see you as a friend. This is bad! The only time you are allowed to invite students out to any event or dinner is if they have graduated. At that point it is okay. If you're still looking for people to have dinner with on a Friday night, ask out your fellow JETs. They are in the same boat as you and are looking for a good experience in Japan and hoping to make friends. Don't isolate yourself or forget about them.

Problem #31: You're being snubbed or ridiculed for studying Japanese

 One of the best co-workers I had used to love ridiculing me for studying Japanese. She would say things like "You don't have to study Japanese. The JTEs can translate anything you want." "You've studied

Japanese for how many years and you can't speak it at a business level yet?" "Maybe you should quit teaching and dedicate your time to the language by going to a language school. You'll never learn it in your spare time." "You'll never speak the language as well as us, so why bother?" These little snide remarks about how I studied Japanese would always grind my gears and leave me a little irritated going into my next class.

We didn't turn a corner to resolving our issue until I sat down with her one on one and spoke to her in Japanese about why it was bad that I was learning Japanese. It turned out the main reason why she was offended was because throughout her life she felt that foreign customs and culture were invading Japan and that Japan was slowly losing its identity. A part of that identity is the language itself and how difficult it is to read and write even for Japanese people. When a foreigner (yours truly) from a well-known country waltzed in and proceeded to improve their Japanese skills, she felt threatened. She felt that Japan was losing one of the qualities that separated itself from the world, the language barrier. For a good three months, she made snide remarks on how I shouldn't be learning Japanese and how if I want to learn Japanese I should be going to a language school and not studying during work hours in hopes that I would stop (even though I finished lessons and my preparations for the next lesson or two). By the way, after the lessons are over, studying Japanese is a part of our job.

Solution: If someone gives you grief for studying Japanese, don't let them get you down. Stay positive and instead of avoiding them, reach out to them. Ask them why you studying Japanese is a bad thing. If they're sane, they'll eventually cut it out and realize you're just trying to fit in and communicate. It came down to me confronting the teacher and letting her know that I was learning the language out of respect for them. I explained how I had friends in Japan since high school and that I desired to get to know them more. I didn't call a meeting, I just calmly sat down with the troubled teacher and discussed our issues and giving both sides an opportunity to voice their opinion (in Japanese). After reassuring her that I wasn't trying to offend her or anyone and that I was only trying to make friends and leave a good impression, she backed off. I think it also helped that I had won over her fellow peers by using the steps I mentioned earlier.

The truth is not everyone is going to like you at the office. But if you can win over the hearts of a few colleagues, resolving issues becomes easier. If you're attacked for studying the language, always take the approach of wanting to communicate and show respect to the locals. If they still persist in bullying you for wanting to learn, they're insane and you should try to avoid them.

Problem #32: Poor communication leads me to uncomfortable situations

While you're a JET, there may be times when you will get taken advantage of unless you establish boundaries. During the summer months there wasn't much going on and I had a lot of free time. One day a fellow teacher asked if I would be interested in performing in the opening ceremony of the summer festival's talent show. I was thrilled and thought it was a sign that students and teachers trusted me after dedicating a full year of service to the school. I asked if there was anything I should be aware of and the teacher said everything would be fine.

I assumed this was going to be a large dance group and likely the size of a class, anywhere from 20-40 people. This was a mistake and the teacher did not properly communicate with me. It turns out the dance group was three boys and two of them had decided to drop out after the leader who was bisexual decided on a song that was extremely feminine. The situation made me feel uncomfortable and a part of me wanted to stop. However, I realized that quitting would've been the wrong thing to do, especially to a young boy who wanted to display his sexuality to his peers and be proud of it. I danced with him and the two of us danced to the feminine song as best we could. My supervisor was pleased and so were many teachers with my decision to support the student in his efforts to proudly display his sexuality. Meanwhile, several of my male co-workers began to question my own sexuality and were distrustful and disgusted at first until I told them to knock it off and that I did it to support the student.

Solution: The lesson I want you to takeaway is to ask questions and push your curiosity when a teacher or student asks you to do something. I'm not saying the Japanese are terrible communicators it's just they are trained to only communicate and share the details they believe necessary to get the job done. If you're curious about anything, you need to ask. Ask about numbers, their expectations, and how they are getting involved. You want to avoid the situation where the teacher in question is forcing you to do all of the work for them or putting you in a position you're not entirely comfortable with. If you do feel uncomfortable, weigh the pros and cons of refusing and how it could affect your students. Remember though that when in doubt, always put your students' well-being first.

Problem #33: Being accused of something you're not

While this is a rare scenario, it did happen to me after I assisted the student in the school talent show. Rumors began to spread around the school that I was gay and even the teachers asked me if I was a homosexual. I am not saying that homosexuality is bad. I have friends who are proud of their sexuality and are finally admitting to it and are now happy for doing so. What the problem is here is when someone accuses you of something you're not and you're getting ridiculed for it.

Solution: In general, you want to avoid topics of sexuality around the work place since Japan is a conservative country. What you believe and support in your home town or state, may not sit well with your co-workers. After the talent show I had to defend my identity as a heterosexual male and put my co-workers concerns at ease that I was possibly a homosexual. I had to keep telling them again and again, that I was straight, (which I am) and that I've had a girlfriend before and that I did what I did to support the student. This is the key I want you to take away. There will be times when you have to put the happiness of your students first and if you do your job well, you'll support your students. Your co-workers might question you and your methods, but if you can support your actions and prove that they were for the good of the students, they should and ought to back off.

Had the problem still persisted, I would've brought the issue to the attention of my fellow JETs and any support group I have to seek their counsel. Then I would've talked about how I was being harassed by my co-workers and bring it to the attention of my supervisor and vice principal and explain why I was upset. Thankfully it didn't get to this stage since I showed anger when people asked me about it, but whatever action you take, always remember you're doing it for your students.

Problem #34: You're being accused of having a romantic interest in a student or worse, having sexual relations with a student

Okay. Let's talk seriously for a bit. Aside from injuring a student or co-worker, this is probably the worst thing you can do or be accused of while being a JET. I nipped this problem right in the bud as soon as someone accused me of it, and the conversation ended thanks to my actions. If you want to protect your job and reputation as a teacher, you need to act fast and with force if someone even hints this is an issue. I'm going to tell you what happened to me, what I did to solve the issue, and give some general tips on establishing boundaries between you and your students.

What happened to me: When I was new on the job, I jumped at every opportunity to help out and get involved in the school. One day, a co-worker who taught Japanese came up to me and asked if I'd be willing to tutor a young female 2nd year student who wanted to study abroad in two months. I was thrilled! I thought to myself "Finally a chance to do my job and make a real difference in the life of someone wanting to expand their horizons."

The female student and I hit it off and after seeing she was serious about studying abroad, we decided to meet for lessons three times a week for an hour. We worked hard, and she struggled with the grammar from time to time, but she was making progress. After a month of our lessons I was experiencing some backlash from a gossipy JTE. It didn't help that our planning sessions were a bit rough with constant adjustments. One day she said, "Adam I think you need to spend less time with your student and more time working on your lessons. What is going on between you two? No one at our school or in Japan for all I know tutors a student that much unless something is going on." Although I calmly explained to the JTE that I was tutoring the student as much as possible within two months before she went abroad, the JTE suggested that I was developing a relationship with the student.

What I did to solve the issue: As soon as I heard those words I knew I had to take action quickly before people started to ask questions. The following week I made an excuse and told my student that due to some scheduling and reassignments amongst the teachers, I only had time to tutor her once a week and I recommended she ask questions between classes or get an additional tutor. Thankfully she took my advice and enrolled in an English cram school for additional support. By the end of her time abroad she spoke near intermediate level English, passed one of the more difficult English entrance exams and got admitted to a private college for foreign language studies. She ended up being the first in her family to attend college. Although our lessons eventually ended when she became a third-year student, we kept in touch and I consider her one of my best success stories.

To solve the issue, I had to set boundaries between myself and the student in question. It doesn't matter how noble you think your intentions are. If you are accused of having any kind of romantic relationship with a student, you are obligated to put those rumors to rest by creating distance between you and the student.

Ways to establish distance between you and a student:

- Limit the number of tutoring sessions to once a week.
- If they wave to you in the hallway, nod and give a quick wave, but don't try to start a conversation with them.
- Don't ask too much about their personal life. If they want to tell you about it let it happen naturally.
- Don't play favorites.
- It's okay to have students meet you during office hours, but don't make any special exceptions.

To end this section, I want to say that how you handle a relationship with a student upon graduating is a different story. I've heard stories of JETs and their fellow students grabbing a beer and celebrating their success and keeping in touch over the years and have even heard of a crazy story or two of a JET marrying a student five or seven years later. The important thing is that as long as you are working as a teacher and the student is in your care, you have to keep a professional distance between each other. After graduation, you do what you want.

Problem #35: I'm not sure where I'm allowed to eat lunch

When I first began my job as a JET, I was told that I was only allowed to eat at a specific time and it had to be at my desk. This was done as a controlling method because the JTEs weren't sure how to manage me. I followed the rules at first, but then when I was stepping outside during lunch hour to talk with my supervisor on our way to a meeting, I noticed a teacher walking back carrying their lunch.

I commented on how delicious it looked and then looked at my JTE supervisor and asked, "Are we allowed to eat outside and purchase food from across the street?" My question made my supervisor sweat a little since she wasn't sure how to respond, but the other teacher thankfully said "Why yes! Of course! As long as you're back in time for your classes."

Eventually I learned that just because someone tells you, you can't do something, doesn't make it true. When it comes to lunch hours and little rules, do what everyone else does. Thanks to the realization I could get cheap food from across the street, it saved me an extra 30 minutes of preparation time in the mornings, which while I didn't realize it at the time, would really help me once I became overworked.

When you eat lunch, follow the rules and don't take too much time to do it. You could also eat lunch with your students and sit by a different group each day like I did for the first two months. This allowed me to break the ice with them and start memorizing names. Lunch hour is extremely useful both for lesson prep and also for relaxation, but how you use it is up to you.

Problem #36: You lose all of your lesson plans on the school's PC.

This happened to me in April and it put me behind for a little bit. While I don't know what other programs schools use for their computers, the Board of Education in Tokyo has a special system in place for PCs and they can monitor your activity. Well one of these system methods is that any teacher who leaves the school and gets transferred, will have all of their files deleted on the PC they used at the school. This is done to maintain privacy and allow the computer to be used by a new incoming teacher. Just to provide you a backstory as to why teachers would leave and why a system was established, every year in March, several teachers transfer schools since they have finished their contracts. Unlike in America where teachers have the possibility to stay at a school for their lifetime and just keep renewing their 1-year contract, Japan has a limit of five years for the average teacher unless they are a music teacher, or valued highly by the school for their actions. My school's history teacher and basketball coach was the exception because he had seen my school through dark times and so had remained in the service of the school for more than 10 years. Meanwhile the majority of teachers will be placed in different schools because the board of education believes it is "good for them and will help them grow." Anyways, the teachers who transfer out leave their laptops behind, and during my first year as a JET, I was using my vice principal's laptop since he didn't want it and the Board of Education was slow to provide me my own.

When my vice principal transferred to a nearby school, he left his laptop behind and little did I know that all of the data on his laptop would disappear. This included all lesson plans, all documents, everything I had written and used for the classes up until now. You can probably imagine my shock when several semesters' worth of lesson plans, data, and information just disappeared overnight. I was saddened by it, but since then I've learned from my mistakes. Here's what you can do to prevent this from happening to you.

Solution: First, start a filing system when you arrive at the job and whenever you make a handout or worksheet. Save the copy on your laptop, print out a solid copy, and keep it neat so in the event you were to lose data, you could easily make several photocopies. If you want to be sneaky, you could take a flash drive and transfer all of your files after the semester ends really quickly. While USBs are not supposed to be used at the school, if you must you have to sign special permission to only use them. What I noticed is that USBs can't transfer files over to the work laptops, but you can open them and print them off if you want. Another tricky solution is to use the guest account available on those laptops. I noticed that the guest account on my mini laptop never got reset and so I was able to reuse some of the worksheets I made previously. If you want to try it, save some of the documents to your guest account in addition to printing off and saving hard copies and see if it gets reset the following semester. If you have your own personal laptop, none of this should happen, but believe me it's better to be safe than sorry. Finally, when in doubt, ask your supervisor if all the computers get their data reset every April.

Problem #37: You are not allowed to use a USB flash drive or outlets for personal use other than the work laptop.

This is an issue you're likely going to face when you're a JET and while there is no real solution around it due to the rules and regulations set by the Japanese Board of Education, I feel it's necessary you understand why this rule is in place. The reason why you're not allowed to use flash drives and USBs is due to an incident around 20 years ago. A high school math teacher fell behind his grading, so he thought he would continue working at home late into the night. He transferred his students' grades to his flash drive and took them home. At some point either between returning home for the evening or returning to the school, the flash drive fell out and was lost. Worst part, someone took the flash drive and for whatever reason, made the final grades of various students public on the Internet. Ever since the incident, the Board made a rule that no flash drives were allowed in the schools unless signed for official use by the vice principal.

If you want to use a flash drive, explain to the vice principal why you need to use it and approach him with another teacher whom you can trust. Sign the review document and transfer whatever files you need. If the vice principal is not present due to a meeting at another school or they are just not present for the day, you may have to bend the rules and use your own flash drive. Just be discreet about it and don't let anyone catch you.

This other issue which personally I think my JTE was just doing this to grind my gears, is how teachers are not supposed to use the electrical outlets in classrooms and the faculty room for personal use. The reason why she brought this up was because I was using my phone as an alarm for an active game in the class and needed to charge it since it had been in use the entire day and would otherwise die in the middle of the last class. Thankfully the JTE didn't bring this up until after class, but she said teachers and students are not meant to use the outlets unless they are doing so for educational purposes. The local families pay for the electricity bill of the school so my JTE argued that the students and teachers were stealing money from the residents of the area by using the outlets when we're otherwise not supposed to. I thought her argument was hilarious because every day I'd seen her charging her own phone and listening to podcasts while she worked.

Other teachers would be doing this as well and students would use the outlets in classrooms to charge their phones.

If a JTE gives you grief about using the electrical outlets in classrooms and the faculty room, just nod and say you understand and humor them. As long as your co-workers are using the outlets for their phones, feel free to use them as well. This could be a mere passive aggressive behavior play on their part to just make you miserable, but if you're worried about it, just cover your iPhone with a book while it's connected and don't let anyone see you using it. If the same person still gives you grief about the issue and how you are possibly breaking the rules, tell them that maybe they ought to bring up the issue at the next faculty meeting. Tell them sarcastically that they should enforce a hall monitor to wander around the faculty room, classrooms, and the hallways during lunch hours and reprimand anyone who dares to use an electrical outlet. I guarantee you, they won't because even they know how ridiculous of an idea that is and they will be very unpopular amongst their colleagues. This is how I solved my problem: sarcasm, politely nodding my head and agreeing, and just ignoring the irksome JTE.

Problem #38: A co-worker is angry at me for something I did. Help!

Every school has a culture and that culture is going to impact how the teachers make decisions and how they want their students to act. I was still learning my school's culture when I accidentally offended and angered the school basketball coach whom I was assisting during the practices. During my first year I was assisting both the boys and the girls basketball practices. The girls had very few numbers and were upset that they never had enough for a 5-on-5 game. I thought it'd be a good idea if I could get three of the boys to participate in one of the practices to let the girls team have the experience of a match. The boys were on board with it since the teams met on different days, but the basketball coach was not. In his mind, allowing three of his players to play with the girls would "soften" them and they would lose their edge in the upcoming games. He warned me to never do that again.

I was shocked as to how offended the basketball coach was at my attempt to provide a 5-on-5 scrimmage for the girls' team. But it was also against the culture of my school when it came to how boys interacted with girls. As I learned later from a colleague, the way boys and girls are expected to interact here at school were limited on purpose because they're still growing up. To allow both genders to play sports together could lead to possible problems. I was the exception because I was the teacher and could control my actions and behavior, but my students were viewed as delicate and uncontrollable, which is why they were separated in almost all sports activities throughout the day.

Solution: To make it up to my co-worker, I did two things. First, I apologized for my mistake and bowed when I did so. I did my best to not anger him during practices for two weeks and just let things cool off for a bit. Then during the holiday season, I brought in some little gifts from America for the players and the coaches. They liked that a lot and before I knew it, my little error was completely forgotten. If you make a mistake and end up offending a colleague, apologize. I had to learn the hard way in a different scenario that even though another colleague was at fault for offending me, I had to apologize in order for the relationship to continue. The Japanese are a proud race where face and honor mean everything to an individual. If you're waiting for an apology from a Japanese person when you feel slighted, it's likely not going to happen. If you want to resolve conflicts quickly in the office, own up to them no matter what degree you were involved and apologize so life can return to normal in the office.

Problem #39: I am surrounded by negativity in the office

During my second semester, one problem I faced was staying happy and positive on the job. While I knew being a teacher was important in Japanese society and I had the potential to change lives for the better, I was also surrounded by several teachers who didn't care about the job. Being in an environment where you're told you don't matter and the students' futures don't matter, can have an impact on how you value your job and yourself. Two of the main culprits behind my developing lack of faith were the computer technician and my new supervisor.

The computer technician at my school didn't want his job and didn't care about the students. When I tried to make conversation with him he'd constantly complain about the students and how he wanted to go home and take a nap. When I had computer problems he said he had never dealt with PC software problems before and that his former job was being a secretary.

His negative attitude and that of my supervisor which went from serious to not caring and having no desire to plan lessons anymore, made me challenge my own belief in the job.

Solution: When you start getting surrounded by negative and lazy people, I want you to separate yourself from them as much as possible. If you have to meet with them, limit the time and try to be in a different room when they're present. Reporting them is not going to do any good unless they have prevented you from doing your job. Complaining is one thing, but until you have proof they are preventing you from teaching your students, there is very little you can do about the issue.

Problem #40: My co-workers are asleep at their desks. Can I sleep too?

This will probably come as a surprise to many of you when you arrive in Japan because it sure did surprise me when I saw it. Unlike our home countries, the Japanese view people who nap at their desk as hard workers. This would not happen in America. Sure, there are some hard workers who collapse from exhaustion, but most of the time, these people are just lazy and are bored so they decide to take a nap. It's right up there with people "pretending" to work when really, they have nothing better to do.

Personal story: It was my second month at work and I saw my first supervisor falling asleep at her desk. I was worried about her so I woke her up, in fear that she might get in trouble if the vice principal caught her sleeping. I woke her up once and she thanked me for looking out for her. To my horror I discovered her 40 minutes later in the same position, so I woke her up again. This time she grew irritated and said, "Adam we're all adults here. Taking a nap during the work hours is acceptable here in Japan, because people believe it means we're hard workers." With that remark she went back to sleep and used her books as a makeshift pillow. What surprised me from this response was not just that she admitted to sleeping by choice, but that she was also admitting to taking advantage of a system that promotes laziness.

To add to this, I saw increasing numbers of sleepy Japanese in the office throughout the semester and the vice principal didn't wake them up. Even my vice principal took naps at his desk. There are also other articles that can support my claim to this mysterious phenomenon. (https://www.nytimes.com/2016/12/16/world/what-in-the-world/japan-inemuri-public-sleeping.html). Other Jets in Tokyo started to follow their peers and take naps during the work hours, but let me say this, the GOOD employees don't do this. While your boss might not say anything to your face, they will complain to the Board of Education. During post development training we had the head of the conference tell us that several schools complained about JETs sleeping on the job and asked everyone to stop. Even though sleeping is a part of the work culture and the Board of Education is unaware of this problem, it is a bad habit JETs should stay away from. The teachers I respected the most and who gave everything they had to the job never took power naps. They remained vigilant and awake regardless of their age and busy schedule.

Solution: If you take a nap, you do it at your own risk of being scolded by the Board of Education. In my opinion sleeping on the job is also a bad habit to get into if you plan to eventually return home where sleeping at work is frowned upon. Remember you're at the school to represent your culture and society, so make them proud and take the high road. JETs should have the least amount of work given to them, so if you're not getting enough sleep at home, something is wrong.

Problem #41: You're accused of wrong doing or breaking things

I was unfortunate to experience this on occasion at my school, but like I said, not everyone's experience is the same and hopefully you will have a better experience. I remember when we were transferring schools and one of the PE teachers told me the custodians said that my locker was broken. I told him the locker had been broken since the beginning and that the only real way to open it was to gently kick the door at the bottom and it would pop open. The gym teacher felt bad that I was dealing with this issue for a long time so he asked the teacher in charge of the move (my new supervisor) who was unfortunately not fond of me. When he was told that I should get a new locker, he insulted me quickly in Japanese saying, "It's Adam's fault for the broken locker and thus he doesn't deserve one unless he wants to buy one". I did not get the locker and I told the distraught and stunned PE teacher that it was okay and that I expected this would happen.

Another scenario was when a JTE accused me of breaking a projector screen since it was one we hadn't used before and she noticed it was broken after I had just finished using it. When I tried to explain how I found it this way when we were setting up, she said that if it was damaged earlier than I should've reported it sooner and so she had no other option than to believe I was at fault. The JTE demanded that I apologize to the homeroom teacher who possessed the screen for breaking it and when I said why don't we do it together, she said she shouldn't have to since she did not touch it. Note this is back when I was being overworked and had very little team teaching support from my department. During lunch I found the homeroom teacher and apologized for possibly breaking the screen, and the teacher just laughed it off. He said his students broke it a long time ago in a previous class after tripping and knocking it down.

Solution: There may come a time when a JTE or another teacher blames you for something you didn't do. Standup for yourself, but predetermine the outcome. If you know that the argument is a losing one and the relationship will only get worse if you don't take responsibility for it, just humor the teacher's pride and apologize. Like I said, apologizing goes a long way in Japanese society, even if you're not at fault for it. In order to prevent this from happening sooner, keep a log or a mental note of when you find broken things and report them to the JTE or teacher who is about to use it.

Problem #42: I'm not valued! "We are Japanese and you are not."

The classic "Us vs. Them" mentality can be really soul crushing after you've put a lot of time and effort into your work and you're not thanked for it. I didn't have to deal with this problem personally, but one of my fellow JET friends did. She was at a well to do school with a good reputation of sending students to top tier colleges. Teaching was her future career and so when she arrived in the JET program, she poured her heart and soul into the job. I have a lot of respect for her and she even inspired me when I doubted the program at times. I believe it was during her second year that the attitudes of her colleagues came to the surface. She wrote in her blog that when you spend more time with your colleagues than you do at home, they become like a second family to you. You know their quirks, ticks, and sometimes for better or worse their problems. During her second year she was overworked like I was and even though she helped plan a major event for the school, she was never thanked for it. When she tried discussing the significance of the event with her colleagues, they'd say snide remarks such as "You're not Japanese, so don't worry about it. It's okay. You'll never understand." There were constant reminders that no matter how hard she worked, she would never fit in or belong with her co-workers or for that matter Japanese society. One of my favorite lines in her blog was how she was tired of hearing the idea that "our tiny little island nation is the best place to live in the world and that you don't belong here." It was the attitudes of her co-workers that eventually made her decide to not renew her contract like I did.

Solution: Honestly speaking, this is a problem that cannot be easily solved by your own doing because it depends upon the attitudes of your co-workers. You're either going to have people in your work environment who respect and appreciate what you do, or those who will take you for granted. What you can do is try to put in the hours and see if people notice. Usually being the last person to leave the office will start generating a buzz about you and your work ethic. But at the end of the day, you need to ask yourself "how important is it to seek validation and be appreciated by my co-workers?" Because in the end, it might not be as important as you think. I would try to leave work early and have fun outside or take up a hobby to prevent your work life from becoming your only life. Remember at the end of the day, your students' well-being and your own happiness are all that matters.

Problem #43: My co-workers seem to be superficial towards me. Why?

This is actually an issue of *honne* vs *tatemae* and this will come up in many forms during your time as a JET. First let's talk about what these terms are exactly. *Honne* and *tatemae* are Japanese terms that describe how a person feels. "*Honne*" 本音, translated to "true sound" is how a person truly feels and is often covered by their emotions or façade they show in public, their "*Tatemae*." *Tatemae* 建前 literally means "built in front" or facade. If you're an Asian Studies major or if you've lived in the country long enough, you've probably heard of this, but if not, sit back and listen.

Honne and *tatemae* have been discussed in hundreds of books and thesis in the United States. A simple google search will generate over 60,000 results.

Here's an example of *tatemae*. You're trying to communicate with a co-worker in Japanese with a simple greeting or even in a mix of English and Japanese. Out of the blue a co-worker, whom you've never spoken to or maybe just joins in the conversation says something to the equivalent of "Wow! Your Japanese is so good." I'm serious about the "wow" part. When you hear it the first time, of course you'll naturally feel happy and pleased with the compliment, but then it happens again, and again, and again even from locals whom you've never met before.

You bump into someone on the street and say *sumimasen* or "excuse me" in Japanese out of respect when suddenly the Japanese person turns around and says "Wow you speak really good Japanese." After a while one can't help but feel coddled or looked down upon like a child in some scenarios. Another one is where you're making lesson plans, you're putting your heart and soul into making the perfect plan with objects and details and the JTE says "wow, you've really improved as a teacher." Then when the time comes the JTE doesn't use your lesson and they don't take you to the classroom.

As you listen to this contradiction, you can't help but feel like an outsider and you might feel a little weird. How you react is up to you, but the reason why the Japanese behave this way is because…they don't want to insult you, they want to show they support you even if you make a mistake, so they don't know what else to do other than compliment you on the effort instead of the result. They might think your accent is funny, or you pronounced a word wrong or maybe you said a profane word by accident but they don't want to laugh at your mistake. They may even wonder why you keep making lessons despite their intention to not use them since you're not a licensed teacher.

Solution: You have two ways to go about this. You can get upset that it's hard to have a working relationship with teachers in your office because they don't want to extend a Japanese conversation outside of "Hello! Wow your Japanese is so good." This might lead you to view the Japanese as superficial, which I don't recommend you do, but believe me I've harbored those feelings before. Or, you can keep your head down and keep trying to extend the conversation or add in a new piece to the lesson plan and I guarantee you that before your time is up as a JET you will see progress. The most extreme example I know of was when a JET wasn't invited to team-teach until after seven to eight months of being at the school and sitting at her desk. She had already decided to quit the program four months in, but at the very least she got to teach once. Like I said this is the extreme scenario.

Whatever you do, don't be afraid to get angry in private and vent your frustrations. There will be some locals who no matter what you do, will refuse to view you as an equal even if you speak Japanese and have a Masters degree in the subject. Here's an example of a conversation I had with a local on my way back from the convenience store on a sunny afternoon.

Me: "Hello Ma'am." (in Japanese)

Japanese woman: "WOW!" (literally said wow in English and made a big deal out of it by throwing her arms in the air like a cartoon character) "Your Japanese is so good!" (She began to clap her hands).

Me: "I'm sorry? All I did was say hello though." (in Japanese)

Japanese woman: "I'm sorry. I don't understand English." (in English).

Me: "but I'm speaking Japanese." (in Japanese)

Japanese woman: "YES" (in English) … (runs away.)

I promise this will be a normal conversation you'll have, hopefully without the running away part. It's okay to get upset and feel frustrated while you're trying to make your way in a society that is homogenous and trained since birth to treat outsiders differently. Just keep the frustrations to yourself and vent in private.

Problem #44: I feel trapped at the office and have no outside outlet

We need to face the possibility that we might not feel appreciated at work all the time. Even though the JET program has an astounding reputation, a lot of schools are entering the program for the first time and don't know how to properly interact with a foreign colleague. As a result, no matter how hard you work you might feel trapped or worn down.

What do you do? Even if you love teaching and it is your pride and joy, I want you to go out into the world wherever you are and find a hobby. There will be days even at the best workplace, where you're going to feel terrible and having a hobby or outlet to turn to in those dark times can really help.

When I had a majority of the English department no longer team-teaching with me and I had to come up with a majority of the lessons, I began to search for outlets to not only take my mind off things, but to also make me happy and set boundaries between work and my life. I started to play videogames, then I learned how they were made, and then I went into YouTube and video production. Little did I know that my little hobby would lead into a possible career after the JET Program so I'm thankful I did it.

Solution: Set some rules so you can have boundaries. For example, unless you have a major deadline or lesson due the following day, don't stay at the office past 6:00 pm. Always schedule some downtime to relax and explore the area and also time to pursue a hobby at your leisure. Don't cross your hobby with the JET program, and always make the JET program a priority, but it's good to start thinking about your happiness and also possibly a future career after JET. Remember, you can't be a JET forever.

Problem #45: I don't understand how sick days work!

Sick days is one of the most discussed topics amongst JETs. The situation is different for everyone and it will depend on whether you're working at a public or private school, but I'll give you the situation I faced when I was working in Tokyo. As a JET I was first allowed to take as many days as I needed off as long as I successfully worked 16 days and met my work quota. If I suddenly became ill, the school could rearrange my schedule so long as I was able to fit 16 days each month. This was an amazing system for the first few months until I received vacation days.

Six months into my time working as a JET I was given 10 days of vacation. Now if I was sick I could still take a sick day, but the new rules in effect caused it to cut into vacation time. My schedule could no longer be rearranged since I had received vacation days. Once the summer arrives, you get an additional day off in August. In the second year you earn 11 days off, 12 days for three years, 13 days for four years, and two weeks for your 5th year. If you miss work when you don't have enough vacation time, your salary will be deducted at an hourly rate.

Problem #46: Co-workers are jealous of your schedule and salary

While this isn't supposed to happen because your salary should be a secret, there have been cases where a JET was harassed for how much money they were earning. The truth is that you will likely have more freedom and fewer responsibilities than most of your fellow co-workers. When you're spotted not panicking over work or working on the next major report, and not having to attend the meetings despite earning just as much as a full-time teacher, it is only natural for people to get jealous. It's especially bad if those feelings carry over into the classroom and impact your team-teaching.

Solution: **Never ever tell anyone at the school how much you make**. The truth is you actually make more than the beginning teachers and some other co-workers there. The last thing you want is for people to get upset and refuse to work with you because they know you make more money than they do without experiencing their pressures and responsibilities.

Problem #47: I feel like my colleagues mean something different when they talk to me. What is this underlying meaning?

Ah yes! The hidden meaning to requests. What I'm about to discuss next is rather cultural and a difficult task that everyone will encounter regardless of how long they've studied Japanese. The challenge is how differently the Japanese language is spoken and the structure of it compared to other languages. For example, in English we tend to be blunt. We say what we want, and we communicate exactly what we need at the time. Japanese on the other hand tends to be a softer language that takes into consideration the feelings and rank of others which is why different forms and degrees of speech affect sentence endings. Because of this tendency, what a person truly wants can often times be shrouded within a delicately spoken phrase or sentence. In order to preserve the person's honor or to imply a message, the speaker depends on the listener to take in the information and act accordingly. In short, while English can be taken at face value, Japanese should be taken at a slightly deeper level.

Here's an example that is probably a little more obvious. Situation: two co-workers are sitting in an office on a summer afternoon. Person A is a higher-ranking officer than Person B.

Person A: "Wow it sure is hot in here isn't it."

Person B: "Sure is. I heard it's going to be even hotter tomorrow."

Person A: "Ugh. Yeah, I don't want to go to work tomorrow."

Person B: "You should take the day off if the boss will allow it. Ha-ha."

Note: (The two remain in their chairs, but person A is slightly agitated at person B)

This is your typical office banter and it seems normal on the surface with the exception of Person A's irritability. But why? Let's translate this conversation a little more in depth.

Person A: "Wow it sure is hot in here isn't it."

(Hidden meaning: Hey do you mind turning on the air conditioner? I don't want to seem selfish for ordering you to do it, so I hope you'll agree with me and want to turn it on).

Person B: "Sure is eh. I heard it's going to be even hotter tomorrow."

(Person B is oblivious to Person A's cry for help).

Person A: "Ugh. Yeah, I don't want to go to work tomorrow."

(Hidden meaning: I'm really suffering from the heat and would really appreciate it if you could turn on the air conditioner since you're closest to it).

Person B: "You should take the day off if the boss will allow it. Ha-ha."

(Person B is still oblivious).

Person A is annoyed and slowly walks towards Person B and the air conditioner.

As you're reading this I guarantee every JET has been Person B at least once. I know I've been guilty of this once or twice and this has led to some frustration with my co-workers. They had to pull me aside and teach me this cultural aspect of Japan so I could communicate effectively. Here's what happened at my office.

Me: "Hello Ms. Yamaguchi. Here are the worksheets and the description of tomorrow's activity as you requested."

JTE: "Excellent, I'll be happy to chat with you next period about our plan for tomorrow."

Me: "Sounds great! Thank you very much."

(1 hour later)

JTE: "Wow! Adam the activities look fantastic. Would you mind putting these in a lesson plan format so I know what to say?"

(Hidden meaning: I'd really appreciate it if you would make a very detailed lesson plan for now on when we do activities).

Me: "Sure thing!"

The way we used to teach was that I would run the class for the most part and give students a lot of exposure. I thought the JTE would only want me to teach for a little bit, so I believed a lesson plan wasn't necessary, since I only had 15 minutes to teach something. What I didn't understand was that the JTE really wanted a lesson plan for every lesson for now on after that day. Other teachers told her to mention it to me since I didn't pick up on it. There was a good two weeks where most of my fellow English teachers were annoyed at me and I didn't understand until I asked my supervisor why. That was when they educated me on the importance of understanding the hidden and subtle meanings within the Japanese language.

Solution: To avoid and eventually overcome situations like this, tell the JTEs and other teachers when you first meet them that although your cultures and languages are different, you're eager to learn their thinking and way of life. Ask them to point out cultural mistakes you might make. Never consider yourself the expert even if you have a degree because I guarantee you will make mistakes and it's best if you walk into the situation and admit you're oblivious. Because I mentioned my credentials when we first met, my fellow co-workers gave me the benefit of the doubt so I was pleased at first, but when I didn't pick up on a cultural cue, it led to frustration. Everything began to resolve when I told them to freely point out directly or pull me aside when I screwed up.

Problem #48: You're trying to get out of a social event you don't want to attend

When you're just getting used to being the local celebrity, it is easy to get overwhelmed with curious onlookers, invitations, and people being very open to you. Sometimes though you might make a mistake or forget you have an obligation or you're just really tired and don't feel like going to that dinner social you promised people. However, you are expected to attend any and all events you RSVP to. I remember when I was invited to a dinner by my fellow first-year teacher and I was excited to go at first, but then learned that the other JTE whom I really didn't get along with was also attending. Wanting to avoid an awkward dinner, I tried to back out of it by saying a night course I enrolled in had a due date the following day so it was doubtful I could make it.

The teacher who was organizing the event said it was not a problem, so I felt relieved. BUT, the JTE who I didn't get along with pulled me aside (this is after I requested my fellow co-workers to tell me in private when I was screwing up culturally) and said what I was doing was really rude because restaurants in Japan usually need a group reservation and that the group of 9 might have to pay for my seat if I didn't show up. It was a good lesson for me to learn and so I made a compromise and told the organizer that I could make the first hour but would then have to leave. I noticed she brightened up a bit more when I told her that instead of me having to bail completely. I persevered through the ordeal and left a good impression on the host. After that night the host and I were speaking to each other more often and she included me in other events.

Solution: Know your limits for when you are being invited to social events. Don't be afraid to say no and offer to reschedule an event. I even had a teacher who could tell I was overwhelmed by all of the events in the beginning of my first two months and suggested I decline invitations on occasion. Be sure to set aside time for yourself to relax and enjoy the country. You don't have to be at everyone's beck and call. If you do end up RSVPing to an event and you don't want to go, only attend for half of the event. It's better to go for some of the event and be polite than not show up at all.

Problem #49: My teachers won't let me into the meetings

You're excited with your job and learning new things every day. Your job couldn't get any better, but one day you learn that the other teachers do not want you to attend the faculty meetings. You start to panic and think perhaps they're talking about you in private, or that they don't see you as a real teacher. So, you're left in the faculty room or left to watch club activities.

Solution: I want you to calm down if this is your concern because believe me when I say the faculty meetings aren't what they're cracked up to be. They're not serving tea and sweets at these and often times they're quite boring. The purpose of the faculty meeting I went to was to discuss upcoming events, policy changes, budget, or perhaps issues that need to be kept confidential. The meetings are completely in Japanese, so unless you want to go there to practice your listening skills, there is really no benefit to you attending. The one time I did attend a faculty meeting it was about school uniforms, upcoming policies, and what really happened to two students who ended up in a hospital due to their stupidity. At least six teachers were dozing off and I was tempted to as well.

Your time is better spent either remaining in the teachers' room so you can watch over people's belongings and thus allow teachers the opportunity to return to their desk if they forget something. You could also spend time at club activities during these faculty meetings and sometimes that's what I did. Because I spent my time with the girls basketball team, they stayed alive much longer despite lack of numbers and enjoyed practice. Overall, I felt more useful to my school being the odd man out. If you do feel offended, don't, because likely they didn't want you at the meeting out of fear that you would be bored.

Problem #50: How do I dress for work when some teachers wear shorts and T-shirts?

This ties back into the culture of your school. As I said earlier, everyone's situation is different and each school has their own culture that you must adapt to. My situation was slightly unique because although I was instructed at first to dress up in cool business attire, I learned that I was causing some of my fellow co-workers to feel uncomfortable since I dressed better than them. The issue was that I would wear nice shirts at first and the occasional suit and tie, while some of my co-workers who were viewed as the main teacher wore jeans, T-shirts, and even shorts. When your own assistant looks better than you, you've got a problem and I recall the vice principal who was really welcoming pull me aside and say "Adam you should take care not to dress too much for class." After that I changed my clothes based on the teacher I was with. For teachers who wanted to dress more formally, I tried to match them and for those who were more casual, I dressed down. Although I still got gruff on occasion for trying to match the teacher, I always did my best to make the teacher look better than me since I was the assistant.

Solution: When classes begin first take the attitude of a cool business attire and prepare to teach. As you observe other teachers and see how they dress for the first two weeks, try to fit in by perhaps dressing down a little bit while staying somewhat appropriate. When I taught with casual teachers, I always wore jeans and a golf shirt while I dressed a little more formally for other instructors. How you dress will also depend on the reputation of the school. If the school is viewed as one of the area's elite schools, you can bet everyone will be dressed up whereas in a lower level school, the rules will be more relaxed. Go with the flow and you should be just fine. Whatever you do, don't wear anything that is lowcut or has holes in it.

Problem #51: I'm stuck inside the office during the summer and bored out of my mind!

This is one of those annoying scenarios someone in the JET program always complains about. "It's not fair that I have to stay at the school for 16 days a month during the summer. Teachers back home were allowed to leave school and have vacations during the summer, why can't I?" Okay I hear you loud and clear and totally get it. But here's the deal. This is Japan, the club activities meet year-round and there is a set schedule in mind with the Japanese that you likely won't pick up until you've been in the country long enough to understand and "play the scheduling game". If you're smart with your time, *__you're not supposed to be at the school for 16 days a month during the summer__*. SHOCK!

In fact, it is silently expected from your fellow co-workers that no one is going to use their *nenkyu* or vacation days until the summer season begins which is late August. The school year is year-round on a trimester basis with classes ending for the summer season in late July. As a result, you almost have an entire month where you're scheduled to work for 16 days. Problem! There are no classes, everyone is bored, restless, and dying to get out. So here are some tips on what you can do. Warning, some of these are not entirely professional and are borderline edgy, but I'll start with the brilliant ideas first.

Tip #1: Leave work one to two hours early each day and use hourly *nenkyu*. Truth is you can take *nenkyu* or paid vacation by the hour and this was a popular tactic. I even used it a few times despite only having five days left. Leave by 3:00 pm and this way you beat the rush hour traffic back home, and you have the entire night to party! But if you're in charge of a club activity, be sure you show up and take care of your responsibilities.

Tip #2: Go to a restaurant with fellow co-workers for lunch. At my school staff were allowed to leave the premises and get lunch outside when there weren't any classes.

Tip #3: Take three days off (Tues, Wed, Thurs) and use your special one day of summer vacation leave as well (Fri) so you get a nice mini vacation. This will allow you to come into the office refreshed and allow you a good week or two to catchup on making lessons for the fall semester.

Tip #4: Read a book and play with legos. Okay maybe ditch the legos, but that's what I did while I was stuck in the office. My new vice principal was relaxed about it and I made a dragon which I said would be used to decorate my desk and act as a conversation starter for when students visited me. A lot of the teachers I worked with were just catching up on reading during this time.

Tip #5: Join clubs and hangout with students. I know some JETs who joined the swim club and several clubs simply because they could.

Tip #6: Teach your fellow co-workers some English for fun. I remember doing this during the summer when I first arrived and it really helped break the ice. In short, Netflix + Big Bang Theory or any kind of comedy + Japanese subtitles = amazing.

In summary, summer is the best time to use that *nenkyu* which you've hopefully been saving up. Make sure you are caught-up on your lessons for at least two weeks so you've got a nice buffer as the school year begins.

Section 5: Trouble with JTEs

This section is dedicated to dealing with individual problems that come up with your JTEs in the office. We all know that JTEs are great partners and good people who mean well, but sometimes having different cultural values can get in the way of your goals. Let's try to solve these problems quickly and get back to work.

Problem #52: You can't get an English Club started because the JTEs block your attempts

This was my problem during the first semester. I remember when a few students complained that they didn't focus on conversational English in the classroom. I first tried to show there was interest by having some students come with me to the office. The teachers were stunned there was interest since our school was known for not having the most active students when it came to academics. After a lot of talks afterschool and discussion, we decided that adding a conversation section to the classroom wouldn't fit in the curriculum. On top of this the last time an English club was founded, it failed within two months so no one had an interest in starting one again. As I recall it was also a bit of a taboo topic since one of my good colleagues and another JTE tried and couldn't get the club to work.

Solution: While the tables did turn and I was dragged into starting an English club after a JTE wanted some merits attached to his name, I would've taken a different approach instead of just giving up like I had. What I should've done is meet with students anyway. Just because you can't get official backing by the teachers and financial support to run a club, doesn't mean you can't search for a classroom or open space in the building and just chat with students. If I could go back, I would've started from the ground up and gathered a small group of people to speak English with. Meetup once or twice a week after school and chat for an hour or longer depending on people's schedules. Remember, just because you can't call yourself an "English Club" doesn't mean you can't meet on your own terms in school and converse in English.

Problem #53: JTEs challenge your English and disagree with your definitions

This was a surprisingly frequent problem I faced and so did a few others who were not "English" majors or who lacked a degree in ESL teaching (English as a Second Language). It wasn't meant to be a personal attack against anyone's character, but rather part of an ongoing discussion involving English education in Japan. The issue is that the English taught in Japanese classrooms is very formal and restricted to phrases and grammar patterns that are not used in native conversation. Most of the phrases are written for people who want to study English for the purpose of passing the university entrance exams. The language itself in America and your own country has changed compared to English education in Japan, so how you speak and use English might be different compared to what everyone else is used to.

There were multiple occasions, sometimes per day, when a JTE would ask me about a particular English vocabulary word that is either never used anymore or I've never even heard of. Often times the JTE would challenge my definition because the way I used it was not in a dictionary or they believed I mixed up a word.

Solution: Try to not take offence at being questioned, challenged, or corrected on occasion. The JTEs are simply trying to improve their own English and find a common ground to possibly make a connection with you. Smile and embrace it. If the JTE challenges you and says outright you're wrong out of anger or frustration, do not shout back. The last thing you want is an outright argument or fight over a word when you have bigger fish to fry. You can do your best to explain what the word means and how to use it, but if the JTE is too stubborn to accept your explanation and refuses to listen, sometimes the best thing is to simply nod your head and say "Ok. You're right. Thanks for teaching me," and move on. Some things are worth fighting for and others are not.

Problem #54: JTE refuses to meet with you

This is often a misunderstood situation that can become a long-term problem or be solved in an instant. For most of you, it will be handled without any issue, but it will depend on your attitude. The truth is if you feel as though your JTEs are ignoring you for whatever reason, you're probably right. They are ignoring you, but the truth is, most of the JTEs and teachers are overworked, so you're probably the last issue or problem on their mind. Almost every instructor is placed in charge of a homeroom class or some kind of duty with the school be it student discipline or managing the facilities, and then they have their own classes and club activities that depending on the school will run late into the night. I'm guessing that 80% of the time, the JTE or teacher in question is just trying to survive and make it through day to day without having a lesson or deadline blowup in their face.

Solution: If a JTE tells you they can't meet with you, do not take it personally. There are two things you can do. One way is to leave a post it note (please use non-red ink since some teachers fear red for some psychological reasons) and greet them, tell them you're hoping to find a time to chat about the lesson and tell them anytime works for you (ANYTIME MEANING EVEN AFTER 5:00 PM BEFORE HEADING OUT THE DOOR). Now hopefully this meeting takes place a day or two before the lesson because you may have to make adjustments to the lessons if they want to change something at the last minute. Tell them to write you a post it note back so you can set up a time to chat. The second option is to check their schedule to see when they have a free period and then approach their desk and ask in person if they have a chance to chat now or later in the day. If you go down this option though, make sure you're not interrupting a meeting they might be having.

HEADS UP: Before meeting with the teacher, have a proposed lesson plan that shows everything the JTE is meant to do at which time and in the order, your roles, what the students will do, the goals for that lesson, and a detailed explanation of each lesson activity on a separate sheet of paper. This way the teacher can look at it while you explain it quickly in detail and then you can decide if there is anything they want to change. The teachers in an average high school are often overworked and given more tasks than they can handle. Don't take anything they say personally. You just need to find a way to squeeze into their busy schedules. On the next page you'll find a sample lesson plan I made for some JTEs while I was a JET.

Sample Lesson Plan

Time	Name of Activity	JTE	ALT	Students
5 minutes	Greet the students	Takes attendance Asks the ALT what the plan is.	Write the plan for today on the board. Asks a few students how they're doing.	Listen and answer questions.
15 minutes	Grammar Review and Reading	Go over the recent Grammar from chapter 5 and have students repeat after the ALT.	Listen and make sure students are paying attention. When the reading begins come to the front and recite the verses.	Pay attention, take notes, and read from the book while repeating after the ALT.
10 minutes	Boom	Explains the rules with the ALT via demo (see Boom explanation sheet for details) and	Roleplays with the JTE and participates while keeping track	Listens to the rules and passes the ball while using the target

		participates. Asks students English questions when they're caught with the ball.	of the time. Says Boom when time is up.	grammar from the workbook.
10 minutes	Gesture / Picture	Explains the rules with the ALT and makes teams.	Sets up the board while explaining rules.	Break into teams and either using gestures or drawing a picture, conveys the word.
7 minutes	Pop Quiz	Explains what the quiz is and drills the students.	Walks around and makes sure no one is cheating.	Take the quiz.
3 minutes	Saying Thanks and Ending the Lesson	Bows and says goodbye to students.	Bows and says goodbye to students.	Thank teachers for a fun class.

Problem #55: Experiencing passive aggressive behavior from your JTE or your supervisor.

This is the worst problem I had to deal with during my second year on the JET program. My second supervisor ended up turning on me nine months into the program. I remember that we often hung out and spoke in English during our lunch breaks. Today I have a bit more understanding as to why our relationship went south. I really want to address this issue because an employee you respect who suddenly turns on you without warning, can be a real punch to the gut. You might even start questioning yourself "Am I a bad person? Did I offend someone to point of deserving pure hatred?" No one should have to feel this way. To put future problems at ease and to settle the score with my own demons, I'm going to share with you a bit of my story.

Personal story: During the summer months after we all successfully moved into a new school building, I noticed my supervisor was avoiding me, kept conversations short, and refused to speak in English for fun. At first, I brushed it off because he was placed in charge of transferring everyone to the new building and was probably just busy, but once the school year began and he refused to meet with me about the upcoming lessons, I knew we had a problem. Little did I know this was only the beginning. As time passed he became more unprepared for the lessons, would say "ehhh I don't feel like meeting right now or talking about the lessons".

He forced me to do all of the work, refused to read lesson plans and merely placed them back on my desk just to ask "So…Adam what are we doing today?" He would say nothing in class, refused to translate my easy English instructions like he used to and even had the audacity to text on his cellphone in the back while I taught. Due to the one-sided efforts on my part to teach, some lessons fell apart and while I did translate my own English into Japanese, he told me to stop. My hands were tied.

After much deliberation I invited him to a private room to talk one on one and told him I couldn't help but feel that there was a rift between us over the past few months. My supervisor ripped right into me. It turns out he didn't approve of the message I was giving students in class and how it reflected in my teaching. When I pressed him on the matter, he refused to go into detail. He then said my English classes did not cater to his students' abilities. He told me to grow up and that I was not progressing as much as I could to be an ideal teacher in his eyes. We ended the meeting with him saying how he also hated my handwriting, so he quickly lost a lot of respect for me in the office. However, he did tell me I'm good at teaching solo and that I should have more confidence.

I took his advice and complaints to heart and did my best to meet them, but the relationship continued to deteriorate. He still tinkered with his phone in class, gave me death stares in the hallway, passed the wrong handouts in class, canceled our classes multiple times so he could take a day off and go to seminars, which I discovered he could've attended on any other day when he wasn't teaching. Clearly, he wanted nothing to do with me and it was impacting the progress of our students and it showed when we did the reading practice exams and class activities.

In the back of my mind, I always wondered why he suddenly turned on me so I sought the counsel of four fellow teachers. This was a mistake because I should've kept it private, but when the needs of my students are being ignored and their education is at risk, I'm going to complain and seek help regardless of whether or not I hurt someone's feelings.

Why this happened: My fellow co-workers who supported me did some research and spoke with the supervisor on my behalf and we discovered a couple of issues. Eventually I learned that the attacks on me weren't exactly personal, and it all goes back to the old cultural issue of Americans being direct while the Japanese favor the idea of "reading the air" 空気を読む *kūki wo yomu* and reacting to it. The truth was two reasons. The first was that my supervisor was dealing with a lot during the school year outside of moving everyone into the school building and couldn't tell me out of personal honor. I'm guessing the reason was because he volunteered to be my advisor and for the past few months he had been failing for that matter. It got to the point where I had to take care of all handouts and process JET paperwork around him and email people of interest if I wanted things to get done on time.

As for his personal issues, it turned out he had to commute more than two hours one way to school and back home. That's more than four hours in transit on a train. Time was against him and he was also placed in an awkward position that he had hinted, but never really got into until I probed a little deeper. It turns out that despite our age difference of 20 years, he only had two months more experience in the classroom compared to me. This was because his former career in business didn't go as planned and teaching was merely done to make ends meet. It was merely a case of him burning out and no longer having the time to be my advisor and guide me in the lessons. My supervisor followed the Japanese tradition of not exactly saying what he wants to say in hopes I'd figure it out. Unfortunately, I didn't understand until it was too late.

What I did: It wasn't until the post development conference that I learned that pride is one of the greatest treasures to the Japanese. It is one of their most admirable traits, but can also cause problems. I sat down with my troubled supervisor, and told him I was sorry I did not meet his earlier unvoiced expectations and that I would do my best to meet his expectations in my final semester. He said coldly, "Let's see if you can put your words into action and that it's not just idle talk." I know in each other's eyes the other was at fault. I viewed him at fault for being rude and not working with me as a team-teacher and likewise he viewed me at fault for not taking more responsibility and not being able to read his expectations as is the Japanese tradition in the workplace. Knowing this was going to be a losing battle for me since neither side was willing to compromise, I tossed my pride, and apologized for not meeting his expectations. From that day forward, he began to participate and help more in the lessons. I still did what I always did and even volunteered to help other teachers who I wasn't responsible for in my last month. Aside from volunteering, my behavior didn't change. All I said was sorry.

He still passed out the wrong forms on occasion, but I learned to come prepared to class with extra copies so it wouldn't happen. Then he requested I teach extra classes during my final month in March, since he had nothing left to teach and wanted to use my educational games. While I forced myself to stay late until 9:00 and sometimes 10:00 pm at night at the school, I met his demands and quit my job with my head held high.

Solution: I will admit I wish I could've changed a few things now that I'm back and have had time to reflect. First, as soon as you feel that a co-worker is avoiding you or treating you unfairly, it usually means you've done something wrong and they want you to figure it out. Yes, this is implying that you are at fault. This is a common tactic amongst the Japanese in business and the workplace and it involves the person at fault "reading the air" and figuring out they've done something wrong. The Japanese expect Americans to do this without a fault and this is why some problems escalate from a small flame into a wildfire.

Once you sense something is off, spend a week to try and guess what the JTE wants or what you may have done wrong, but if you're absolutely stuck, ask the JTE privately and get to the bottom of the issue. Don't wait for three months like I did. You may or may not get chewed out, but at least you're taking steps. If you know for a fact you are meeting their expectations and yet they are still giving you grief in the classroom and are impacting your students negatively, you have every right to report them after a month. At which point you should go to the vice principal for help. It may come to the point where the three of you (vice principal, JTE in question or supervisor, and you) will need to sit down and talk about some issues. If a meeting does occur, come prepared with a list of grievances the teacher pulled on you over the past month. The problem teacher in question will most likely have complaints of their own so this is the appropriate time to calmly voice all problems and let the JTE voice their own side of the story.

No matter what happens, don't make this a shouting contest or an argument where the other is at fault. Try to make this a learning experience on both sides where all problems are placed on the table and you can resolve them and get back to teaching. If anyone challenges you on why a JTE not wanting to work with you is a problem, state that it is impacting your students and I guarantee you'll win the dispute and your reasons for the meeting will be validated. If you're upset because a former friendly colleague turned on you and you want to make amends, that is beyond the role of the vice principal. Let me emphasize that you should only be reporting the issue to the vice principal and requesting a sit down **if your students are being affected**. Friendships are not the primary issue at the workplace.

Problem #56: JTEs want you to take on more responsibility than what is required or suggested of an ALT or CIR

This was the second reason why my supervisor turned on me in my final year as a JET. He was burned out and because he was tired of all the responsibility placed upon him, he wanted me to take additional responsibility and that included making full lessons and teaching a class with no support. In other words, my supervisor thought it was time for me to go from assistant teacher to having the responsibilities of a full-time faculty member. He mentioned this to me in passing during one of our meetings and I didn't really understand his intention at first until I looked at our problem objectively. I will admit being offered more responsibility isn't necessarily a bad thing. Most people would be jumping for joy, but it's not a promotion and it's not additional pay. In this scenario what the teacher is asking, is for you to go beyond your role of the JET Program.

Solution: If you wish to accept additional responsibility in your school that's fine, but understand you will most likely not be compensated for it. There have been JETs who have become a full club leader for a sport, led an English debate team to national championships, and have gone above and beyond the call of duty of a JET. This is a good thing, but before you take on this responsibility, I think you need to first ask yourself if you're willing to do this and if being a teacher is what you really want in life. I want you to ask yourself these questions because the JET program doesn't lead to a permanent career. Depending on how you use your time, you could segway into teaching back home or continuing down the ESL route in Japan, but it would be outside of the JET Program. For those of you who want the experience of working in a foreign country, but don't necessarily want to be a teacher afterwards, you might want to be taking classes or developing skills in preparation for your next job. Whatever path you choose, once the offer and request for you to carry on the work of a full-time Japanese employee has been placed by a supervisor or JTE, you need to chat with the vice principal, and the person who requested it and go over your contract. This is a conversation that deserves a positive discussion and you should only do what you feel comfortable with. Be honest with how long you were thinking of staying on the program and your future career aspirations.

Problem #57: JTE leaves me alone in the classroom

This is an important issue that you could come across in your time as a JET and if you don't solve immediately, could potentially lead to legal consequences against you and the JET Program. This is when you are left alone in a classroom full of students.

I know, you might be thinking, WHAT?!? How is that illegal? Unless you've gone through Japan's standard education for becoming a licensed foreign language teacher and have the certificate, you're likely not qualified. Yes, being a JET does not automatically qualify you as a full-fledged instructor. Since you're not a fully trained and provisioned instructor by Japanese standards, you are at risk of putting the JET program in harm's way. If a fight were to break out, a student had a heart attack or if anything bad happened and you were the only adult in the room with the students during this time, the parents of the harmed student would do a couple things. They'd be angry that a real sensei by Japanese standards was not present to handle the situation and you would be blamed and so would the school. Not only that, but the JET program could also be put at risk and you can bet that if a student was injured enough to be hospitalized for whatever reason, it'll get national attention. Keep in mind though, this rule only applies to classroom hours, and not afterschool.

This sounds panicky, I know, but believe me when I say that schools will look after themselves first and the JET program second. I remember a group of 3rd year students were taking a vacation abroad and got injured in a traffic accident. They were too young to drive in the first place and they used fake IDs so it got the attention of the national media. My school was panicking and they did their best to hide the fact that it was their students in the accident so they told the teachers that anyone who asked the whereabouts of the students was to lie and say they were on vacation or visiting colleges. The point is, you do not want to be involved in a negative national news story. Another incident was when a JET brought a relative to Japan and the relative started a brawl in the bar with the JET present. People were injured, it got attention of the news and the JET program was put on the spot causing people to judge the character of foreign instructors. Like I said, you do not want to be the center of these stories. If you're a licensed teacher by Japanese standards and want to outrank your fellow JETs and be viewed as an equal amongst your colleagues, then that's a different story and you can feel free to take the brunt of the blame, but most of the JETs I doubt will want to take this chance.

Solution: Here's how to avoid it. Always enter the classroom together with the JTE you are partnered with for the day. If you have to set up for class that day, set up early, and return to the teacher's room and walk back up with the instructor. If you feel comfortable and 100% confident that the teacher will arrive on time, you may enter the classroom, but whatever you do…do not start the lesson without the teacher present. If a teacher asks you why the class wasn't started by the time they arrived, explain to them that legally you are not supposed to since you're not a qualified instructor. Once you've achieved the teaching certificate of a Japanese instructor, you should be able to disregard the rule.

Problem #58: JTE undermines you in the classroom

Before I dive into this story, I need to say that just because you have conflicts with a JTE, doesn't mean you can't turn it around. By the second half of the program this JTE and I smoothed things over and had several successful classes together.

What happened: For my first eight months, my appointed supervisor and JTE whom I mainly taught with and I were at odds with each other. There were times she would yell at me in front of the students, belittle my worksheets, apologize to students for a mistake I made with writing instructions in Japanese (by the way there were no mistakes), blame me for faulty equipment, provide different instructions in the classroom and interrupt my lessons. In the end, we had to come to a rather large confrontation with half of the department to put an end to our ongoing dispute.

What you can do / what I did: Talk to another teacher you feel comfortable with and ask for advice. Only talk to one teacher, not several. Keep a log of all the offenses the teacher did to you and be ready to provide it in the event of a sit-down confrontation. Next, I want you to sit down with yourself and try to take a neutral side to this scenario. Try to write down what happened from an objective point of view without taking sides and placing you as the victim. Actually, write it down and write how you feel when you do this. Try to see if the other JTE has some merits to what they say. If you can justify your actions in a calm, neutral manner on paper and in a meeting, you're golden.

The biggest mistake I made in handling this problem was that I waited too long to confront my supervisor. It was getting to the point where student discipline was starting to collapse and the students asked me privately why I never got along with this specific teacher. I mentioned this issue to a fellow teacher whom I confided with and so we made a plan for me to talk about student discipline with my supervisor in English and she would listen privately. When I told the JTE that our students were questioning our relationship in the classroom, she laughed and told me to stop making our classes a popularity contest. She then continued to explain that 70% of our students in the class had mental disabilities which is why they behaved poorly. When I asked for the list of students with disabilities in the classroom she said the list was only available to "real teachers." She ended the meeting by saying, "Adam I know the students and other people think I'm bossy, but I don't care and neither should you. They're just kids who don't know what they're saying." After the JTE / supervisor in question left for her next class, the teacher who acted as a witness said, "yeah she's not seeing the problems you both are facing in the classroom." That was the moment when the teacher told me to bring the issue in a departmental meeting to put an end to it.

I asked my new supervisor (if you haven't guessed, I got a new supervisor when the new semester began) with the head of our department for permission to hold a meeting. First, I told my side of the story and then the JTE / my old supervisor in question was called in and told her side of the story. Finally, we were both called in and then we ended up apologizing to each other. I know you're thinking, "Wait. Adam why were you apologizing? You did nothing wrong!" It's true I didn't, but not in the eyes of the Japanese teacher. By the way, get used to apologizing even for tiny offences you may feel you're not responsible for. It goes a long way in maintaining the *wa* 和 or "harmony" in the office. In our meeting the teacher admitted that the bulk of her behavior was her way of trying to make me improve as a teacher since I wasn't meeting her expectations. I listened to her comments, told her what I would work on, and said I would rise to meet her expectations and go beyond, but would appreciate criticisms to come after class in private and in a calm manner. Ever since that meeting took place, my relationship with that JTE took a complete 180. Our classes rivaled my favorite teacher's classes with regards to fun and positive outcomes.

The takeaway: Don't be afraid to speak up if you feel you've been mistreated, but be aware that you need to approach the meeting in a neutral standpoint with facts, dates, and other details. Keep in mind, that you might also be a part of the problem without realizing it. Confrontation is a last resort technique since Japanese people don't like confrontation and if they lose in an argument, they lose their personal honor and face. However, if the students begin to suffer because of your poor working relationship with a JTE, you need to step up and get it sorted out. At the end of the day, your interactions with the students and what they get out of your classes is the most important thing. Your relationship with the teachers comes second and sadly sometimes last. You're there to teach and enrich the education of your students, not to make friends with your colleagues.

Section 6: Trouble Beyond the Office
When you live in a place long enough, you're going to be developing relationships and being active in the community. There will be problems you'll encounter in your daily life and you'll want them to be resolved smoothly so you can enjoy your time abroad. While this section isn't necessarily focused on teaching, I hope it will come in handy and give you some street sense.

Problem #59: You bump into your students in the middle of the street
Uh oh! You're wearing something inappropriate or maybe you're with friends and you don't want your students knowing about your private life.

Student: "Hey Mr. / Mrs. _____. Let's go shopping together!"

Solution: Greet them politely and wish them a fun time, but tell them that you cannot spend time with them until after they graduate since the public and other teachers might misunderstand if they see you two chatting outside school. This is true because although you are placed in charge of them at school, in public it's a different story. There must be boundaries between you and your students. They can't know your address or private contact information. As fun as a day with your fellow students might sound, it just wouldn't fly with society until after they graduate. If the student in question is one of the opposite gender, immediately put distance between them. If the student seems hurt by your actions in class, pull them aside and explain why it is inappropriate for a student and teacher to be spending time together outside of school. I've had to do it a few times and every time I explained it, the student understood and we cleared some misunderstandings when they thought I disliked them.

Problem #60: You've been given an opportunity to make some extra money while you're on the JET Program. What should you do?

Woo hoo! Who wouldn't want more money especially in these expensive times? However, you're under contract with the JET Program and you're legally not supposed to accept any kind of monetary compensation outside of the program for risk of being fired. You've been given a really cool opportunity to make some extra cash on the side of your current job and you want to take it, but aren't sure what to do. Believe it or not, I too was in a similar situation.

My story: Remember those hobbies I was telling you about? Back when I was looking for something to do that would give me comfort, I turned to video making. I started a YouTube channel and really enjoyed making movies (I still do). One day, my computer battery died and my laptop refused to turn on. I took a day off from school to visit a computer shop which little to my knowledge turned out to be the headquarters for MSI Japan. I explained how I was looking for a computer shop, but was completely lost, and so they helped me out and told the clerk I was coming. On top of that, they invited me to an MSI gaming party where players could challenge professionals 1 on 1 for prizes. I jumped at the chance and enjoyed an afternoon of snacks, good company, virtual reality showcases, and the chance to network with professional gamers and individuals in the Japanese gaming industry. One of the people whom I hit it off with turned out to be a marketing representative for MSI and said she was looking for YouTubers to make some unboxing videos. I really wanted to jump at the chance, but remembered my contract rules about making money on the side.

What I did was I told the marketing representative that I would make the video for free. I wanted the exposure and challenge of making a video in a foreign language and so I volunteered and explained the predicament of my contract. We agreed that although I wouldn't make any money, they would give me MSI products as a thank you for the video. The video was a lot of fun to make although time consuming with the editing, I would've done it again in a heartbeat.

Solution: You have a few options when it comes to being given a monetary opportunity outside of JET.

A. Accept a non-monetary gift. Perhaps something consumable or useful.
B. Just volunteer your services for free and take it as a learning experience.

Before you even accept the work, make sure it won't interfere with your current job as an ALT, CIR, or SEA. Option A is technically not illegal. Option B is the safest bet, but make sure that your priorities are with the JET Program.

Problem #61: How do I get through post development conference:

Ah yes, the dreaded post development conference. That awkward time when you reencounter friendly faces from the orientation whose names you've probably forgotten since you were scattered all across the area. But if you've been doing a bang-up job of keeping in touch, you've got nothing to worry about. Even so, there's likely assigned seating, you all have to come up with lesson plans, and listen to how you've been messing up in the classroom and hearing the glorious scenarios and lives of the rare well-placed JETs where they teach philosophical debating in English while you're just getting past "I'm fine. Thanks, and you?" It can be a frustrating time and I guarantee that by the end of it, you're going to wish you didn't have to attend these. However, after experiencing two of these events, I'm going to give you some advice on how to make the most of your time there and enjoy it.

Tip 1: Do your best to take it seriously and before it starts, write out a list of problems you're encountering at the school and what you'd like some help solving. Doing this will give you some conversation points to talk about when the JETs break into groups on problem solving.

Tip 2: Let your vice principal and other JTEs know about your conference and that you'll be out for three days. The vice principal of your school should get a memo about the event and you will be paid to go and this counts as your work days. Don't let anyone else tell you otherwise. Be sure to let the other JTEs know so they can properly prepare their own lessons in your absence.

Tip 3: Don't just zone out during the presentations. Although some school scenarios won't apply directly to you, you might find a way to incorporate a strategy or technique a JET used indirectly to one of your activities. For example, I remember one of my friends and fellow JETs had to prove his usefulness to his JTE so he made art to show to his students for each lesson to illustrate a point. Now while I'm a terrible artist, I had a feeling that students liked being creative and the creative works of others. This in turn inspired a new game I brought to my students called "Gesture Picture."

Tip 4: Try to make the activities fun and engaging. If a JET representative asks you to do a bit of roleplaying, change it up a little bit to make it fun for everyone listening. Here's an actual example of when the JET representative from the Tokyo Board of Education called on me for roleplaying to teach the suffix "**-ing**"

BOE member: Daisuke, what are you do**ing**?

Me (Daisuke): Me? Oh, I'm drink**ing** beer.

(audience laughter)

BOE member: Ummm Daisuke, drink**ing** is not allowed in the classroom. You're too young.

Me (Daisuke): Sssshhhhh don't tell sensei. It's go**ing** to be a secret.

BOE member: Daisuke. I am the teacher.

Me (Daisuke): Oh yeah! Well, would you like some?

Tip 5: Do not make any sexual jokes during your presentation. I remember we had two male JETs teaching a mock lesson to the entire room and they titled it "Twerk Master 5000" you can imagine that the BOE members did not understand, but the JETs were appalled and a little uncomfortable when they had to possibly act out sexual moves. Thankfully we didn't. In short, don't do that or anything you feel would make the JETs or anyone feel awkward.

Tip 6: Go eat lunch with the other JETs. Everyone is looking for people to hang out with and if you see someone by themselves, invite them. They'll appreciate it. I know I did when JETs invited me to lunch even if they were total strangers.

Tip 7: Join a group to hangout or do something fun afterwards with so you have something to look forward to. When I was there a group of guys and gals were planning to go roller skating after the second day. We talked about it on day one and we planned it accordingly. We had a great time and it was a great way to blow off steam and we had something funny to talk about going into our third and final day at post development.

Tip 8: Try and help other JETs by contributing to the conversations and giving advice where you know it will help them. If you just sit there zoned out staring at the clock, you're going to feel like a zombie. Don't be that person!

Problem #62: Whether or not to renew your contract

This is a situation you're going to encounter within your first three months as a JET. It's a beautiful fall afternoon. You're working at your desk making a lesson plan when suddenly the vice principal walks over to your desk and explains how the Board of Education needs you to make a decision regarding your employment the following year. You can either choose to remain for an extra year or you can decide not to stay an extra year in which case you will be forced to return home and leave the JET program by July. A roller coaster of emotions goes through you. You might feel homesick, you might feel like you haven't really gotten a firm grasp of the culture and your life abroad and you're not sure what to do. The tough part is, you have to make a decision within two weeks. This is not a lot of time.

Back in my first year as a JET, I didn't have to be asked a second time. I knew instantly that I wanted to sign up for a second year and the vice principal was really pleased. Sure, there were some problems I was facing, but I knew they could be resolved over time. My family situation was fine and I still was searching for what I really wanted to do with my life. I had no idea that it was all going to change for me personally the following year. It's true I left the program early to look after my family and pursue my dreams, but I stayed until the end of the school year during my 2nd year as a JET.

Solution: My advice to you is this. Unless you're regretting going to work day in and day out since arriving, you've put yourself out there with no good results, you've already got a job lined up back home and you know exactly what you want to do with your life and you have a plan, stay on for a second year.

This is my one super pet peeve with the JET program. The scheduling is arranged so that everyone has to make a decision by October and November because that is when the new round of applicants for the JET program begin to apply. The program needs to keep a tally of current JETs and applicants. As a result, the program is designed to force out people who may not have had the opportunity to settle in and really give Japan a chance. So dear reader if you're reading this right now, I highly advise you to stay for a 2nd year and give it a shot. It's makes it easier on the scheduling for the school and you're more likely to leave your mark and find something about Japan you truly enjoy.

Problem #63: How do I prepare for the next step in life while I'm a JET?

Perhaps you've decided that being a teacher isn't exactly for you or this is the year you won't recontract. Whatever your reason, you need to start thinking about your next steps because life continues after the JET Program. Do you remember those hard questions I asked you at the beginning of the book? Well it's time for a new set of hard questions.

1. Do you want to work in Japan or back in your home country?

166

I think several people take their current position in JET for granted and they should ask themselves "which country do I want to work in?" Consider the life you've made in Japan so far. Do you have a loved one or are in a serious relationship with a local? Do you prefer the friendships and lifestyle you've made for yourself while abroad? Do you have any obligations to attend to back home? Can you handle additional demanding tasks in a Japanese work environment where you will likely no longer have as much freedom as you currently do?

Make sure you are weighing the pros and cons for staying in Japan as I did when I was beginning to consider not contracting for a third year. Asking yourself all of these questions and making a list is going to put the rest of your experience in perspective and cause you to make decisions on how you either want to enjoy the rest of your time abroad or settle in and attempt to make a permanent home in Japan. Whatever you decide, make sure you settle on a home base first and then proceed to question number two.

2. Do you want to go into teaching or an entirely different career?

You already have experience being a teacher so perhaps you'll have an easier time finding work, but what if you want to pursue a new career? For those who want to pursue teaching, you'll likely be limited to only teaching English in Japan and if you want to teach at a high school or college level, you'll need to get a teaching certificate online or at a formal school. If you're wanting to teach in Japan and pursue a new course, you will likely have an uphill battle proving your speaking ability. But it is possible, so my recommendation is to stick with ESL at first while you start knocking out some of the necessary requirements. If you want further assistance, ask some of your fellow co-workers what they did in order to become a fully licensed teacher in their field.

To be a teacher in the United States, you will need some classroom experience as a student teacher, an additional degree and a teaching certificate. Then you'll need to find an open position. I think you'll have more opportunities in the United States to pursue any kind of teaching, but ESL might be difficult since you'll be limited to language schools.

For those wanting to pursue a new career outside of teaching, make a list of what you like and don't like and talk to your friends and family about it. If you've been working on a hobby that you enjoy outside of JET, perhaps see if you can use that as a springboard into a new job.

No matter your position and opinion, ask yourself...

3. Do you need additional education or training to help with employment?

Further education is not a bad thing, but consider the amount of money you've hopefully been saving up while you're a JET and if you'll have enough to afford an apartment. Is there a specific school you'd like to join or one that is known in your future field to pump out the top applicants for jobs? Make sure you have the time, money, and support to pull this off regardless of what field you're getting into.

4. Do you want to start a business?

Start researching what kind of skills you need and make a business plan. Do you need to live with your folks while you get afloat or can you work on this as a side hustle? I recommend reading "What If It Does Work Out" by Susie Moore if you're considering going down this route.

5. Do you need more time to think about all of this?

If you're still in the JET program and need more time to take a look at all the options ahead of you, don't panic. It's not a problem. Talk with your friends, family members, and other JETs. You don't have to quit your job just yet and sometimes the best option will naturally appear in front of you.

For JETs already determined to leave, the Tokyo Board of Education will provide private career forums for you to ask questions and possibly interview for future jobs that will start after your contract ends in July. Rest assured there will be opportunities to look for jobs.

Problem #64: I want to leave the JET Program early. Please help.

There are times on the job when you'll feel like you just want to quit the JET Program and head back home early. As much as you may want to pack up and leave, it is really frowned upon since depending on when you leave, how you leave, and the caliber of your school, you run the risk of putting your school in a tight spot. Teachers will have to make lessons without you and any clubs you were running or were a significant part of can also run the risk of collapse. On top of all this, should you decide to reapply for the JET Program in the future, you're likely not going to be admitted since the program managers will see that you left and cannot be trusted to commit to your job. It's a sad truth.

While I am not supposed to encourage leaving the JET Program early, I can tell you it is possible. I should know, because I too had to leave the JET Program suddenly about ¾'s the way into my second and final year. Remember those questions I asked you at the very beginning of the book? You know, the one where I mentioned life moves on back home without you and that you will miss some important events and changes. The truth is I hit my breaking point when I received news that my father's health wasn't doing so well and he needed me to support him. I know of other JETs whose family members were close to death and they still didn't leave the program, but just visited instead and came back to school. That's fine, but I knew that I had the chance to make a difference by returning home, and so I decided to cut my time on the program short.

In addition to looking after my family, the reasons for me leaving were growing at the time. My supervisor's passive aggressive behavior grew out of proportion and the bullying seemed to have no end in sight. I was being overworked and was required to make tools for several teachers' lessons late into the night. Slowly but surely, I was developing insomnia with all of the stresses coming down at once so I would only get an average of three hours of sleep a night and sometimes none as I stared at my ceiling. It dawned on me one morning that being an English teacher wasn't the career path for me. My true passion was game development and making YouTube videos and I knew that my current job wouldn't allow me to pursue that career on the side. So I decided to quit. But the way I quit had a big impact on how my school accepted the decision and how it made life for everyone much easier when it came to finding a replacement. Here's a guide on how to quit the JET Program early.

Solution: Step 1: Have a very strong reason and *necessity* for returning home.

My father's health was the primary reason for me leaving while the rest of the reasons I recently listed were just icing on the cake. If you want to leave the JET Program early your reason needs to be health related. One of the JETs whom a teacher at my school worked with just returned home for the holidays and then never came back. The worst part was explaining the reasons over the phone. While I'm sure the JET was happy to not have to return to their job, they left a lot of things unattended to: next semester's classes, closing their apartment, bank account, cell phone, any relationships they may have had…just poof! Gone! That is not the way you want to leave. Make sure your reason for leaving is a good one and be responsible.

Step 2. Schedule a meeting with your JET head

They'll be a JET as well and you should tell them of your intention and reason for leaving. When I did this my JET leader walked me through the steps and gave me some advice on how to approach this without getting scathed by co-workers or just angry people in general. After your meeting ends, tell the JET person if you still want to quit or if you have second thoughts and want to stay. The next step is the beginning of the end if you continue.

Step 3. Schedule a meeting with your vice principal

Remember what I said earlier, the vice principal is the person who makes all of the decisions regarding the major issues at school while the principal is merely an icon or PR person. Tell the vice principal your reasons for leaving and that you'd like to stay until March.

Step 4. Provide plenty of notice ahead of time so your school can prepare.

A smart thing for you to do is to no matter your reason for leaving, is to try to stick it out until March. That is the month when new teachers are brought in, the new semester begins so the classroom lessons are not that intense and your school will have an easier time finding your replacement. I knew my school would be in a lot of trouble after winter break if I didn't stay to the end of the school year.

Although your official JET Contract will state that you only need to provide one month's worth of notice should you decide to leave early, that is nowhere near enough time. Think about it, everyone at your school is busy and it will take some time for the vice principal to come up with the paperwork for you to sign and to confirm with the Board of Education that you are deciding to leave the JET Program. By giving the administration at your school plenty of notice and time to react, you're making their job a lot easier. They will also have time to notify the JET Program to be on the lookout for a JET who requests Early Deployment so they can be brought into your school. I confirmed with my fellow ALTs who worked with me at the school that since I gave my school plenty of time and left in March, my replacement arrived within two weeks after I left.

Step 5. Make a to do list

You're most likely going to have a laundry list of people to notify regarding your departure. You need to close accounts such as your phone, bank and Internet and perhaps visit places nearby you'd like to see before leaving the country. I remember I had a decent sized list and I still wasn't able to complete it. Of course, I settled all my accounts, but I didn't have time to say goodbye to everyone I wanted to nor did I visit all the places I wanted. Leaving early will take time to complete on your own and while you're working, so be prepared to do a lot of leg work.

Step 6. Decide how you want to tell your colleagues and students

This was made into a big deal at the office and people were debating when I should tell my students. The big concern was that the students would want to throw a party for me when parties aren't allowed so we decided to not tell them until the last week of classes. This way students had a little more than a week to write a card or say goodbye if they wanted to. For my colleagues, I told them the truth in passing or if they asked me what my plans

171

were for the upcoming spring break. How you tell your colleagues will depend on your relationship with them, because some people may get offended and possibly harass you until your last day. Thankfully I only had one teacher give me grief for leaving early, but keep in mind the possibility of backlash when you tell people. You also have the option of just leaving quietly without telling your students and colleagues and requesting the vice principal keep it a secret. But if your fellow teachers get wind of it, you're in for a world of hurt. It is best to leave on a good note and let people have a chance to say goodbye to you.

Step 7. Leave with no regrets

By the time my journey came to an end, I was able to hold my head up high and be proud of everything I accomplished during my time on the JET Program. I want you to have the same experience, so go out and fulfill all your duties up to the day you leave. I was at the office to the day before my flight home to help out and have dinner with colleagues. I would've changed nothing regarding how I left as I reflect on it. Japan and the JET Program were great to me and provided me a great learning experience. I plan to revisit Japan in the future and I hope you will too.

Chapter 5: Japanese Culture and Society

I've saved this culture section until last since it is different from surviving as a JET in the office, which was the primary focus of the book. This chapter will cover safety, holidays, making friends, fitting in, and just not causing trouble. One could call these street smarts but they're slightly different. Unlike the kind of street smarts that can save your skin in dangerous scenarios, these are mainly to prevent you from looking like a moron. There are some scenarios mentioned below which can be classified as dangerous, but compared to other countries you will not be facing them as much or at all for that matter.

Safety

I remember when I was first traveling to Japan and my family was freaking out! They were about to lose their son for a certain amount of time and they weren't sure how safe I'd be since I couldn't communicate via phone 24/7. I want you all to be rest assured that Japan is very safe with one of the lowest crime rates in the world and guns are prohibited in the country. They're not allowed to be sold in gun markets and if you do happen to own one as a resident, the police will be calling upon you every month for checkups, inspections and courses you are required to take.

To emphasize my point on safety and put you worrying parents and loved ones at ease, Japan has a unique neighborhood system that is set across the entire country. In every neighborhood within a four to five block distance, there is a police box pronounced as *kōban* 交番. Two officers are manning the police box at all times. One officer is sometimes out on patrol on his bicycle while the other remains inside to take complaints, calls, or help citizens who are lost. They do a great job and in fact sometimes too great of a job in that people have stated the police have to invent crimes to stay busy.

The street next to Rikkyo University's campus. I walked this path every day.

The most likely encounter you will have with a member of Japan's law enforcement is questioning your residence card. I mentioned this earlier in the JET book, but it deserves mentioning again. If a policeman stops you and requests to see your foreigner card or zairyū kādo, just smile and show it to them. The last thing you want to do is start a fight and get into an argument stating they have no right to search you, because believe me, they do. I've had a discussion about foreigners being picked on by the police and although it might appear to be racist or racial profiling, the policemen are the front line for keeping all residents safe. Tokyo alone is home to 1/4 of the entire Japanese population. If they suspect anything or see a face they're not familiar with, you can expect they're going to ask you at least once. It could be as soon as you step off the plane to enter Japan or even while you're shopping with Japanese friends. Do yourself and the officers of the law a favor, and show them your identification documents. Hopefully you should have them, and if you need extra protection, carry a passport with you that holds your permit. If you do not have either of them on you, you're going to be in for at least a four-hour interrogation and then a ride back to your apartment to show you do in fact live there and be photographed so the authorities can keep an eye on you. Long story short, **ALWAYS KEEP YOUR RESIDENCE CARD ON YOU!** Even if you're drinking or just going outside for two minutes to the local convenience store, bring it with you. Too many foreigners' days have been ruined because they were careless. Don't be the next one.

HEADS UP: Ladies, if an officer of the law who is the opposite sex stops you in the middle of the street at night, take some precautionary steps. There have been reports of people dressing up as policemen and stopping women to obtain their phone numbers and addresses. To prevent this from happening to you can do two things. First have them show you their badge which they are required to so by law. Second, you can request to go to a police box to continue the conversation. You have every right to seek aid at a *kōban* and a real police officer will never turn down your request. If they do however, I recommend you run and get into a safe place where you're surrounded by people.

The other major reason you're going to be stopped by police is for riding a bicycle. I know it might sound strange, but most people in Japan commute by bicycle instead of a car. As a result of this cultural tendency to ride bikes, there are gigantic bike storage facilities inside train stations and there are special policies which are rather strict when it comes to riding a bicycle. Personally, I didn't want to deal with the hassle so I never got one, but If you possess a bicycle, you need to have it registered and heaven help you if you borrowed a bike that is not registered to you. If you're caught riding it, the policemen will assume you stole it regardless of your race and they will detain you in the police box (not a cell) until the proper owner has been reached and the facts verified. It's okay to have a bike, but don't lend it to anyone and don't borrow one from a friend, especially not a stranger.

Natural Disasters

Let's talk natural disasters for a moment. I will be honest when I say no place is perfect and that every location has its problems. For Japan, this problem is earthquakes. While I was living in Tokyo I experienced my fair share of them and they were not fun. I remember when I was awakened at 4:15 am on a Monday morning to my bookcase practically falling down next to me. Thankfully I was able to push it up back in time, but that was a 5.0 earthquake. When the JET program begins you will be taken to a special training facility to learn about earthquakes, tsunamis, fires and how to handle them. Be sure to pay close attention and ask questions. If it's a major earthquake, you'll most likely be asked to head towards a public safety spot or evacuation area designated by your ward or district. Make sure you know where that is located so you can go there in the event of an emergency.

Schools have their own way of handling natural disasters and if one takes place while you're working, you should follow their protocol. When I was at my school, every year the 1st-year students were required to spend the night and participate in various evacuation and fire-fighting drills with the local police and fire departments. The sleepover if you want to call it, is a simulation for what they would do if a major earthquake struck the city. Blankets, crackers, and other various supplies are pre-stocked in preparation for the events. On a side note, spending the night at your school's emergency drill is a great way to connect with students. It will also provide you some additional practice should you feel uneasy about coping with Japan's natural disasters. They're quite rare, but earthquakes do happen, so it is best to be prepared. Keep a flashlight, canned goods, bottled water and some non-perishable food in stock at all times in your apartment and you should be okay.

Theft

Theft does happen and home invasions are very rare, but usually involve looting. To prevent this always make sure you lock your doors and windows when you step outside and you should be fine. A quick note however, should you find a burglar in your home as an acquaintance of mine did, you can grab the assailant and hold him in place to prevent his escape if you choose that route, but under no circumstances are you allowed to punch or roughhouse the burglar. Supposedly according to our staff who welcomed us, they said the police would punish the home owner who physically harmed the burglar more than the burglar himself. This is not America, so you will have to learn to keep your anger and emotions in check when it comes to fighting. Self-defense is fine, but if the police think you've crossed the line at any point and injured a person out of aggression, you could face charges despite being the original victim.

Social norms

Ah yes, the one topic I wish almost all JETs were informed of before they joined the program and came to Japan. Let's begin with what I like to call the rules of engagement. Follow these rules and you'll be more approachable and likely to make friends in the country. And who doesn't want friends these days?

The train is arguably one of most frequent ways you're going to be commuting around Japan. So here are some dos and don'ts of the Tokyo Transit System

Do:
- Make very little noise and keep conversation to a small decibel
- Sit in one seat and one seat only (unless you voluntarily give up your seat)
- Give up your seat to someone carrying lots of bags, suitcases, is pregnant, injured, or is elderly
- Space yourself away from other people especially high school girls
- Call out pervs if you spot them
- Keep one hand in your pocket to avoid pick pocketers
- Smush in and get comfy with your body being pressed against other people during rush hour
- Ladies use the ladies only car during designated times (see picture below)
- Put your bags in front of you or above the seat
- Put your bags by your feet when standing
- Move into the open space on the train past the entryway
- Men if you're on the trains and you're within very close proximity to Japanese females, keep both hands visible to as many people as possible in the trains. Keep them on a book or on the hanging handle. Train perverts are a rather big problem in Japan, don't ask me why, but for your school's reputation, you don't want to be accused of sexual harassment. If you're a female, you have the right and privilege to board the females only car on trains to commute to

work and back. This will decrease your chances of getting harassed or touched by any creepy guys.

Don't:
- Talk on your cellphone. (if you have to, then finish your conversation by the time the train departs)
- Eat on the train
- Drink on the train
- Lay across three seats (leave that for drunkards, and you shouldn't be doing that anyway)
- Get too close to high school girls with low cut skirts
- Wear your bag like a backpack. It eats up room on the train
- Crowd the doors
- Elbow someone who is falling asleep and leans on your shoulder

Sign showing female-only train cars.

Other Culture Tips

1. When riding escalators, stay on the right side if you're standing still, and pass on the left. Do not be the moron who blocks both sides talking to their friend. If for whatever reason the sides are reversed, use common sense and follow the natives.

2. Dress conservatively. I know I mentioned this earlier, but I'm going to say it again. Loose clothing is comfy, but you will be judged on how you dress in this country. Especially if people know you're a teacher and may the Gods help you if you're caught outside by your students wearing scant clothing. Women should not be wearing short skirts and short shorts. If you see cleavage in that mirror, you better save that for a night on the town. I know it's rude to say, but it's the custom. Several JETs were given grief for the type of clothing they wore, so do so at your own risk. No shorts at work, unless you're in a P.E. class or participating in a sports festival at the school. Don't be wearing anything with slander on your shirts.

3. Please for heaven's sake don't go to work with purple or blue hair. Your students are going to imitate you and the last thing you want is the Vice Principal or your boss breathing down your neck. Save that for when you get back home in a year or two. I promise your hair will still be there.

4. You're a teacher even outside of the school, so act like one and standup for other students. If you see a student from another school getting harassed by someone, step in, and put yourself between the student and the harasser. I had to do that once and I yelled at a train pervert. Once I mentioned that I was a teacher at such and such high school, he backed away from the student and got off the train immediately in embarrassment. The student thanked me later.

5. Never pay tip. Seriously. Tipping is not a custom in Japan. If someone tries to get you to tip, they're trying to trick you. Don't fall for it.

6. When you're eating at a restaurant, don't double dip.

7. When at a restaurant, do not use your chopsticks to help another person lift up a piece of food who is using their chopsticks. Doing so is a religious offense. Using chopsticks with another person to lift up food is only done so at a funeral or wake.

179

Gaijin smash

Ah yes, Gaijin smash. The widely spread Internet term for people interested in studying abroad to Japan where a foreigner, a.k.a. a *gaijin* 外人 enforces their will on the Japanese to get their way by feigning ignorance of the local customs and traditions. Other definitions define it as a foreigner breaking cultural norms and then ignoring the reproach locals give them. Another definition describes it as where an American pretends to not speak the Japanese language in order to get out of a bad situation. Here's an example, a foreign traveler who is out of cash and trying to make it to the next train, jumps over a ticket scanner and runs past security screaming "I speak a no Japanese. " No one will argue with you. They will likely leave you alone.

Another example is when you are being told to pay for television service as I mentioned earlier in this book and I suggested you say *"terebi wo tabemasen"* which translates to "I don't eat televisions." Gaijin smashing your way to get out tough and sticky situations is good, but when you're doing it to just get something out of selfishness, then I would stop. Simply put, if you're breaking the law with it, don't do it.

How to make friends in Japan

This is honestly one of the most challenging aspects of being a JET. You're at your job almost every weekday and by the time you get out at night you're already wiped. The weekends come and you explore various parts of the city, you travel, and you've got lots of support from your fellow JETs, but then you realize you're missing a social aspect of Japan that you've been curious about. What's it like to have Japanese friends? I was fortunate back in high school since we had a sister city program, so it was easy to be exposed to foreign countries and make friends, especially in a controlled environment. But at age 22-40 you're struggling to get outside your comfort zone and meet people. Well fear not.

I will be honest when I say that it takes a very long time to make friends in Japan and arguably more so than in your home country. If you think about it you have a lot of barriers to overcome. Language barrier, cultural barrier, and the fact that most Japanese people have never had a foreign friend before. Put all of these together and you have your work cut out for you. To get the friends I have today, it took months in order to win their trust and prove that I was a decent person. There's already some distrust towards foreigners due to how the Japanese were raised in a homogeneous society, but you also have lots of news involving violent crimes mainly coming from the U.S. broadcasted into Japanese televisions. In fact, study abroad has decreased over the years due to many Japanese thinking America is no longer a safe place. And quite frankly I don't blame them. Despite all of this, it is possible to make friends if you take the time and are patient.

Tip #1: Frequent a local coffee shop - preferably one with staff members around your age group. When I was first trying to meet people, I had a difficult time at first since I didn't know anyone in Tokyo, but that slowly changed as I became a regular at a local Starbucks afterschool. Almost every day I studied Japanese there for an hour, and I'd always try to make an effort to talk to the staff. This doesn't mean bother them and get their life story and take them for a beer, but talk about the weather or the latest news in Japan. It takes perhaps 30 seconds to a minute and they'll be impressed. Definitely try to do this in Japanese.

It took them awhile to warm up to me, but once they realized I was coming in daily, we eventually got to the point where we could ask for one another's names. Names are powerful since it gives you a sense of familiarity and it's a sign of respect. When you see them again, address them by the name they told you.

In addition to this, it helps if you can visit in the morning before work and before anyone shows up. I find that the staff are more talkative in the morning since they're not running around trying to get drinks poured for 50+ people. Eventually you can work up the courage to ask two or three of the staff out for drinks or dinner. I want you to do two things. If you're a guy, make sure you're inviting a mix of Japanese guys and girls or only guys. Don't just invite all women, people will talk and the last thing you want is for the staff to think you're going after ladies for a quick hookup. For the ladies the same rules apply but vice-versa.

Furthermore, the Japanese have been raised in an environment since birth with very little exposure to foreigners, unless they went to an international school. Making these friendships is going to take time, so don't get discouraged if they say no or feel weird at first. You just got to keep trying to break the social barrier. Once you do, some of these people can be friends for life.

Tip #2: Turn your work buddies into your friends. I don't highly recommend this tip in the beginning, since you're in Japan to teach English and make a positive impact on the community, but sometimes without even realizing it, you'll develop friendships with an entire group. That's exactly what happened to me and they got me through some rough times. I was fortunate to sit next to the 3rd year teachers who were still in their 30's with the exception of one who we viewed as the mother of the group and they began to include me after I learned their names and just chatted for fun during breaks. Learning names is very important, and if you have the opportunity to get food with people you get along very well with (preferably not JTEs) you'll have a grand time. If there is no party planned, take the initiative and invite them out for a quick bite after work. They'll appreciate it and you'll get to know them a little bit better.

Tip #3: http://www.net-menber.com/ Think of this as a meetup group in Japan but for sports lovers. You have all of your basic sports plus a few hobbyist sports and you can sign up to join a team. It was thanks to this website that I got to join two basketball teams which eventually led to other friendships and parties, and BBQs. The teams I joined eventually disbanded since people started careers and families, but for the 10 months I joined them, it was a lot of fun. They should have some requirements when it comes to joining and if you need help translating the website, ask one of your JTEs or another JET who is fluent in Japanese for help.

Tip #4: meetup.com. There are meetups in Japan as well for certain events so you can bet you'll find them. I made a friend of two by attending a videogame event in Tokyo where we bonded over games at a pub. If you're having trouble going out or actively joining groups, try to join a local event that is inclusive. You could take a cooking class or get involved in your local community and network there. What was really cool about living in Japan was the number of festivals that took place. These weren't just major festivals on national holidays, but rather small community festivals. A local neighborhood will typically have a shrine group that will parade a small shrine called an *omikoshi* お神輿 around a certain part of the town or city. If you ask around you should be able to volunteer and perhaps get the chance to help lift the several hundred-pound mobile shrine with dozens of others.

When I was on a basketball team, a lot of the Japanese friends I made who were in my age group loved participating in local festivals. If there was a major holiday with a festival where they could dress up in traditional Japanese garb, they were there. Small community festivals? They were in the front line banging hand drums and bringing forth the shrine to be celebrated around the city blocks. It is possible to get involved. Participating in a festival might be one of the best memories you have during your time abroad.

Tip #5: Making friends with JETs. If done correctly, this should be one of the easier tasks for you as a JET. Everyone is trying to make friends and network, and I know from experience that the friends you make at the opening conference and training can be difficult to keep track of since you're all working several miles apart. Here's what I want you to do. First before you even arrive in Japan, join your area's Facebook group. As soon as you meet them and if you're hitting it off, add them on Facebook. Also take the initiative and advertise events you want to attend to the Facebook group and the friends you make. It can be hard to be a minority in a foreign country so definitely use the Facebook group's functions and events held by your area coordinators to meetup with JETs.

The importance of studying Japanese

Ladies and gentlemen, I can say with confidence that learning Japanese before you arrive in Japan to start your career as a JET is highly recommended. If it were up to me, I would make it a requirement for getting into the program, but that's not the case. There are several reasons why you should study Japanese.

First it shows that you care. You shouldn't expect to have everyone cater to you just because you can't understand them. In Japan, rank and social class are very important. By not studying Japanese and using a translator during your entire stay while though not rude, you're not putting yourself at their level. By not studying Japanese some people may think you believe yourself too good to learn another language. Since many Japanese people are intimidated to speak in English they're going to be scared to talk with you, so being able to speak will calm things down.

Furthermore, if you speak the language around the office, the staff are more likely to include you in activities and treat you as an adult, rather than an ignorant child. I remember when I had to prove myself to them multiple times that I could speak. After the general consensus was that I could understand the comings and goings of the office, I was able to overcome social barriers and communication hurdles much faster. My Japanese even helped two people at one point. One time was when I witnessed a woman having her head nearly crushed in by a truck on the street and ordered locals to phone the police since my phone was dead. The other was when I found a student bleeding from his head and had to call a teacher over for emergency.

It goes without saying that speaking Japanese will allow you to make friends much more easily, but you'll also start to see and think things differently. The Japanese language in general is vague from time to time since they don't always use the subject and the subject is often implied in the conversation. You might hear a normal conversation and understand everything they're saying with the exception of the subject because it is a topic that is of importance to both members in the conversation. It's not that they're trying to keep it a secret from the world and prevent eavesdropping, it's just the natural way of speaking. You'll start seeing things from a different perspective, you'll begin to take into consideration one's rank, honor, and intentions and how they size you up when speaking. What I'm trying to say here is that your mindset will begin to change for the better the longer you study a foreign language, so go study Japanese before coming to Japan. Start today!

Religious organizations / cults

Imagine you're walking downtown minding your own business when suddenly some Japanese people maybe your age, maybe of different ages come up to you and ask if you're lost. You say you're not, but then they complement your Japanese, you feel flattered, one thing leads to another and you're having a pleasant conversation. You begin to think, "Yes, finally I'm making friends and communicating with the locals in Japanese." These people want to keep in touch with you and they say how friendly you are, so they invite you to join one of their religious sessions at a local Buddhist temple or Catholic Church on a weekend or weekday when you're not busy.

STOP STOP STOP! Think for a second. What have I told you up to now when it comes to Japanese people and foreigners? No one in their right mind is going to approach you in the street unless they are forced to speak with you through a work relationship, or if they want something from you. That group's behavior alone is considered improper etiquette. The Japanese people like their space and privacy and are usually shy, so why are these people suddenly eager to invite you to an event after just meeting you on the street?

Well the answer is because these people as they will explain to you, are part of a local Buddhist sect. There are hundreds of these organizations across the country, and while the people are usually nice and friendly, they slowly manipulate you into donating large sums of money due to your participation in events in order to repair the roof or doors to their temple. Then they will ask you to distribute fliers specifically to other foreigners in the hopes of recruiting additional members. Recruiting members gives you more benefits and if this doesn't sound like one fancy pyramid scheme with a big smile on its face, then I don't know what does.

Before I was a JET I had the opportunity to study Japanese for 10 months in Tokyo at a local language school, and our instructors specifically ordered us to report any sightings of these groups near the dorm or the school. The fact they specifically target foreigners to deceive them is insulting, but also a danger to anyone studying abroad or visiting the country. Don't let these people ruin your time. Here's how:

Give them a fake name. From all of my conversations with these people, they don't usually ask for your name until they mention the Buddhist temple group they're affiliated with. I mean if you think about it, if they actually showed a hint of compassion towards you, they would ask for your name first before mentioning the group. Use their conversation tactics to your advantage and provide a fake name, email address, and whatever you do…NEVER EVER give them your LINE instant message contact on your phone. That contact info in general is usually considered sacred and private in Japan, and to tell someone that info means you trust them. Don't go giving it away. They will harass you and they can tell when you've read a message, thanks to LINE's wonderful coding structure. Lastly if you see others being harassed by a similar group, help them get out of a jam. I've done that a few times with foreigners being harassed by two or more Japanese locals. The worst I've ever had to do was raise my voice and threaten to summon the police for harassing a foreigner. That usually scares them away.

Gaijin Hunter

Whether you're a boy or a girl you will encounter these types of people and it's up to you how to act accordingly. A gaijin hunter is someone who will actively latch on to you for your foreignness. They seek out foreigners for multiple reasons.

1) Status symbol: Due to the homogenous society the Japanese were raised in, befriending a foreigner and being seen with them in public boosts their status. They might friend you just to look cool. This type is very difficult to distinguish, but you'll know if they're really there for you when you can rely on them in a time of crisis.

2) English tool: A very common type of gaijin hunter is the type who wants to get free English lessons. I've had my fair share of dealing with this type. Some reveal themselves after a long period of time and some immediately. They ask if you could meet them in a café to teach them English, or they'll just sit right next to you in a café while you're trying to relax and start playing 20 questions. Which isn't a bad thing until they ask the question if you'd be up for meeting them twice a week for English lessons. Why? Again, English is viewed as a social upgrade. Most Japanese people can't speak it very well. Yes, this is generalization, but ask anyone in Japan and they will admit very few can. Even in Tokyo!

3) Get out of Japan free card: This is the type of gaijin hunter who is only interested in a romantic relationship so they can leave the country and immigrate. I find this type to be the most dangerous due to possible long-term effects it will have on one's life. It's okay to fall in love while you're a JET, but make sure your significant other is following you for the right reasons.

4) <u>The quick hookup with a foreigner just because…they're "exotic"</u>:
This is usually an aggressive type of gaijin hunter who is looking to
date, hook up, and brag about it to their friends. Yes, a friend with
benefits type of person exists in every country, but these people are
only interested in you because you're foreign. Don't fall for it. Take
your time in building these relationships. That's when the truth will
shine.

Racism

I need to address an issue that most if not all JETs are going to
experience from time to time while they're working abroad in Japan, and that
is racism. It doesn't matter if you're white, black or Asian, you will
experience it in some form. I've had my fair share of racist incidents from
store owners refusing to help me by saying "a foreigner like you doesn't
belong here." "We don't deal with your kind here." To the silent racism that
slowly boils until it's about to burst. Most of the time it will be the slow and
awkward racism which may seem harmless at first but can wear you down
after a while.

This took place before I was a JET, but it left a big stain on my opinion
of the Japanese that took a long time to heal. I was a part of two basketball
teams in Tokyo while I was attending a language school. The first team
known as the Bull Dogs were generous and kind at first, but once they
realized that the stereotype how all Americans are amazing at basketball
wasn't true, they lost a lot of respect for me. My basketball skills were
simply average. In practice during our warmups they made an effort to shoot
on the opposite of the court leaving me half the gym to myself, and when I
messed up in practice, they got angry. I put up with it for a while until the
day we had a beginners' tournament and they refused to sub me in. Even
thinking about that day still hurts. We were ahead by 15 points and they still
refused to sub me in. I had to beg to be let in and only got to play for two
minutes even though I was the only sub they had. Basically, they would
rather play without any subs than have me sub in for them. I left that
tournament humiliated and the following week I quit the team.

Then I went to another team. This team seemed really kind and since I
had former basketball experience they requested I hold back against their
beginning players, which I did. The only time I went all out was when the

coach wanted to guard me and I knew I could have fun. For a good six months everything was great. The team threw me a farewell dinner and told me I was always welcome to come back and play. Fast forward one year later and I got the news I was allowed to return to Tokyo as a part of the JET Program. I was thrilled to be able to play with my friends again except that the leadership changed. The basketball coach who used to help run the group quit and so did several others. The leader of the group made a rule that foreigners were no longer allowed to play and since I was white, I wasn't allowed. When I asked if I could just watch or help out as a manager, I was denied. After I spoke with the leader of the group, I noticed most of the teammates I was with stopped talking to me, almost as if I was a plague of sorts. Some of them would message me, but I lost a lot of respect unfairly because of unknown reasons that caused the leader to turn against foreigners and that hatred carried over to my teammates. Apparently, there was incidents with foreign players while I was away that negatively impacted the team.

What I've learned from my experience, and what I want you the reader to take away from reading this, is that putting yourself out there in Japan is an adventure that will sometimes be a success and other times not. I promise sometimes you will get hurt, but most of the time you will have fun. It's important to not classify the Japanese race just because of the actions of a few people towards you. Sometimes you won't click with people, but no matter what happens you have to keep pressing on and not let the negative things weigh you down and make you depressed. Surround yourself with people you can trust and laugh with and who bring out the best in you, so you can enjoy the time you have working and living in Japan.

Holidays

Halloween: Arguably the most misunderstood holiday in Japan. There is no trick or treating, no respect for one's ancestors and the original holiday of Samhain. Forget getting free candy at stores either. There are no modern day American style haunted houses or pumpkin displays. Halloween in Japan is one big party, or at least it was in Tokyo. On the weekend of Halloween, one can see a large parade of people marching across the city and the night of Halloween is party central in Roppongi. Thousands of people are out in costume hanging about and its utter mayhem. Streets are jammed and the litter is ridiculous. News reports have been covering the issue for the past few years and it damages the reputation of the American holiday and puts foreign traditions in a bad light in the eyes of the elderly Japanese. If you do happen to participate in the festivities, drink responsibly, pickup after yourself and carry your trash back home because public waste bins will be overflowing. Also try to educate the locals about the importance of the holiday and how it is meant to be kid-friendly.

Christmas: Unlike the holy holiday that celebrates the birth of Christ, Christmas is similar to our Valentine's Day in Japan. It's a romantically viewed holiday where couples are encouraged to go out on dates on Christmas Eve and Christmas Day. The emphasis on family is practically non-existent with the exception of the bucket of chicken tradition. What is this bucket of chicken you might ask? Burger King, KFC and 7/11's and in various locations will be hosting a bucket of chicken dinner event. The meal is valued at $50.00 - $100.00 and this is viewed as a commercialized tradition with the family. Turkey is not normally eaten in Japan, so foreigners would often visit KFC to eat chicken instead to remind them of home and celebrate the holidays. The Japanese took note of this weird tradition and thanks to the wonders of television and mass media, the Japanese now love ordering chicken one month in advance to eat on the 23-25th of December. Forget the families, and Christmas present openings in the morning, and church services. Most people will just eat a bucket of chicken and get a gift for a significant other and go out on a date during the holidays. There is also an old and hopefully dying tradition of how women are supposed to be married by age 25 or else they become a "Christmas cake". A Christmas cake is another food tradition during the holiday season, it's like a strawberry flavored cake, but most people don't eat them after Christmas which is why people compare single women to the discarded Christmas cake. By the way, there is no public holiday on Christmas, so don't be surprised if you have to work on that day.

Valentine's Day and White Day:

Holidays take a different shape in Japan. While Japan does celebrate most of the holidays we celebrate in the States, the general customs are slightly different. Valentine's Day is a great example of cultural differences in a holiday. On Valentine's Day, girls make, YES, I said MAKE chocolates for the boys. Boys do not usually give chocolate on Valentine's Day, but rather make comparisons amongst their male friends to see who got the most chocolate.

It is also common for girls to give chocolates to other girls, but usually it's just because they're friends or co-workers. On the topic of making chocolates, while you could buy a box of chocolates from Godiva and other places, it is better to make chocolates since it is believed that by taking the time to make chocolates, you show that you care about the person.

There are three levels of chocolate on Valentine's Day. *Giri choko* 義理チョコ which means you feel obligated to give chocolate to someone out of duty or to show respect to them. A classic example is a student giving chocolate to a homeroom teacher as a sign of thanks or a female employee giving chocolate to their male boss as a sign of appreciation (and perhaps a nudge for a raise). *Tomo choko* 友チョコ: chocolate given between friends. It could be your best friend or someone you just want to give chocolate in hopes of receiving chocolate in return. *Honne choko* 本音チョコ: the chocolate someone gives to a person they have romantic feelings for. This is usually where the girl gives chocolate to the guy, but I've heard of rare occasions where the male gives chocolate to the girl.

While Valentine's Day seems awesome for the guys since they get all the chocolate, the guys must reciprocate on White Day. On White Day which is March 20th, the guys give chocolates (usually white chocolate) to the girls who gave them chocolates. While Valentine's day might be nice for the guys, the more popular you are, the more expensive White Day becomes. And don't think about cheating your way out of it, because if you don't give back to the girls who gave you chocolates, not only is it rude to them, but you might have problems getting them to behave in your future classes if you are their teacher. If you're strapped for cash you could always lie and say you don't understand White Day because you don't celebrate it in your home country, though this trick will only work once. If you've received lots of chocolates and are in dire need of help regarding repayment, use your school's home economics classroom and cook an American dessert.

Dealing with homesickness

Everyone gets a little home-sick from time to time regardless of age. It happens to the best of us. If you ever feel homesick here are some things you can do to cope. First of all, set up a Skype account and talk to loved ones back home. It can be done very cheaply. Next thing you can do is make a care package for someone you love and send it to them. You might even get something back. Write a letter (not an email), an actual letter to someone back home. I guarantee they'll think it's so cool you sent them mail from Japan. You can get postcards at a local stationary store. Next you can try to cook a local delicacy from home and maybe even teach others. Lack the tools or ingredients? Do some shopping and try to cook it at your school or perhaps take a class. Push comes to shove, go to some American style restaurants and enjoy yourself.

Going to the doctor

Hopefully this does not happen during your career as a JET, but should it, there are some international hospitals with doctors who speak English. If you don't go to one of the main hospitals located in the city, you will need to find a hospital that specializes in your type of injury or pain. There are hospitals which specialize in internal medicine, external injuries, surgeries, ear problems, eye problems, mouth problems, and hospice. I remember I had food poisoning many years ago when I was first learning the language and accidentally walked into a hospice. Thankfully, one of the visitors told me using a dictionary that this hospital specialized in terminally ill patients and did not have an ER.

When it comes to getting prescription medicine, you need to pick it up at a pharmacy, and yes pharmacies don't sell food, they sell actual medicines. Be on the lookout for signs that say 薬屋 *kusuriya* or 薬局 *yakkyoku*. If need be you can always ask someone where one is located, but I noticed most hospitals had a *yakkyoku* across the street to make it easy for patients to get the medicine they needed. I remember when I had bruising in my neck from a basketball injury and they had to give me special lotion to decrease the swelling.

Dentist in Japan

Very similar to the situation with hospitals, there are also English-speaking dentists. Dentistry is also amazingly cheap. I had a good teeth cleaning, same standard procedure I would receive in the U.S. for only $30.00 where as in the U.S. it could be $120.00 - $150.00. Just be sure you check the prices online before you go and call ahead.

Getting a haircut

There is something for everyone. Ladies if you are willing to pay $60.00 - $120.00 treatment, you can go to your stylist of choice. If you'd like to find a cheaper establishment regardless of gender, you can go to the local barber inside a train station where you can get your hair cut for only $11.50. No tip!

Chapter 6: Endgame and Wrapping Up the Program

We've finally come to the closing section of this book. Whether you're staying for one or five years, I hope you've enjoyed the JET program and gotten something out of it. Let's close up shop. As I mentioned earlier, due to some family health problems at home, and my growing desire to start my own business and make a career shift, I decided to terminate my contract early by several months. I did it through several steps and I'm going to emphasize that you go about this the long way. Here's how:

Give several months' notice about your desire and especially your "necessary" reasons for leaving the JET program. When I was preparing to leave the program, the head of the Tokyo JETs hinted that I should not reveal my desire to switch jobs to my supervisor or anyone at the Board of Education. The head told me everyone would be trying to pressure me to stay on full-time because it means more work for them and it's supposedly quite a hassle to get a replacement JET so suddenly. This is all true, however, if you give several months of advance notice and leave right after a semester ends, there should be very little disruption within the school's workflow. I accomplished this by providing five months' notice and had a few private talks with the vice principal. I told him that I would stay up to March, the end of the school year so the teachers would not suffer from my absence and the new JET can start right at the beginning of the school year with the incoming first years, which in my opinion is how it should be done. JETs usually enter the program in August, the middle of the year so students may not warm up to them as easily. But by being with the incoming students, JETs will likely have the opportunity to grow with them.

What I'm trying to tell you is provide as much as time possible. If I had only provided one month's notice, I would have had multiple teachers upset with me and the JET program would have been rushing to get a new JET for my school. None of which is cool in my opinion, so that's why I gave almost half a year's notice. On top of that, I left right when a semester was ending, so there were no scheduling conflicts, and teachers had several weeks to adjust their lessons without the presence of a JET. So that's how you should leave if you want to make everyone's lives easier.

193

Time to go home!

Stay in Japan or go home?

By this point in time, you've probably decided your time with the JET Program has come to an end, whether you've been there for one year or five years as a unicorn JET. But that doesn't mean you have to leave Japan entirely. If you decide to get a new job in Japan, you will have to renew your visa and leave the country and then reenter on a visitor status while your office is filing the application for your new visa. You only have to leave the country for 24 hours, so it's not terrible.

But seriously though, you have a lot to consider. Here are some honest to the gut questions you should ask yourself when considering whether or not to stay or leave Japan.

- Do you have a loved one or have you started a family in Japan?
- Do you have more of a solidified social group with natives and other expats in the area?
- Have you considered a career in TEFL? (Teaching English as a Foreign Language)
- Do you have a job in Japan or America lined up?
- What kind of career are you looking for?

- Are you up for working the long hours?
- Are you okay with possibly not seeing your friends and family back home for a year or maybe more?
- Is your visa almost expired?
- Do you have loved ones waiting for you back home?
- Any financial or legal responsibilities you need to take wrap up back home?

There are pros and cons with every decision you make and the longer you stay in Japan, the more difficult it will be to leave. Believe me, I've been there twice. When I was finishing up my language school, I was tempted to quit graduate school and start a career with MacMillan Publishing when one of the high-ranking officers nearly offered me a job after meeting him at a party. I was also in love with a native and a relationship appeared to be in the works, plus I had a great social group with a basketball team in the area. But I gave it up. Why?

The first time I gave it up was because I had already spent $40,000 on a graduate school education (this 10-month experience being funded as well) and I had my friends and parents back home waiting for me. I wanted to close up shop in the United States by finishing my Masters Degree and then get a job through JET with the hopes of staying three years and then getting a job in Tokyo.

Things changed during that year while I was gone. The basketball team I was a part of underwent new management and became anti-foreign. Most of the members and friends I had left. Japanese and Korean tensions were on the rise. The girl of my dreams suddenly got engaged, and most importantly, I had changed without even realizing it. I got to see almost all of my friends again and while I was enjoying my job, I slowly realized that a career teaching English as a second language wasn't how I wanted to define myself through the age of 30. Had I stayed as a JET for five years as was my original plan, I would've been age 31, and likely stayed in Japan to work for MacMillan or another Japanese company. I would have become another rung in the corporate ladder. Nothing wrong with that, but as I spoke with more entrepreneurs and my contact at MacMillan, the more I realized I wanted to fight for my freedom and live a life he had. I also fell in love with editing videos on YouTube and designing video games and so my goal became to start a small company and sustain it. I realized that my dream job doesn't have to make millions. As long as it keeps a small group of people fed and living the lifestyle of freedom, that is enough for me.

My point is deciding whether or not you want to leave Japan to continue your life in the United States is not the type of thing you can decide within a single day. Talk to your friends about it, talk to any mentors you may have, and ask yourself the questions I wrote above. Talk to yourself, think about it over coffee, sleep on it, and make sure you can decide without looking back. It doesn't mean you'll never visit Japan again, but you need to take steps towards living the life you want.

Searching for a job in Japan

When it comes to searching for a job in Japan, the JET program can help. They have career workshops with companies known to recruit exiting JETs into their workforce. There are companies based in the United States, Japan, and a few other countries, so you do have options.

You also have your standard Monster.com, Indeed.com, company websites, and other resources, but a good measurement of whether or not you want to get a job in Japan or even further your education in Japan, is being able to pass the Japanese Language Proficiency Test (JLPT). Lots of places use the JLPT as a measurement of an applicant's listening and reading skills. If you want any job above the service industry like a hotel or restaurant, you will need to pass the JLPT N1. So far, I have passed the N2, and the exam is offered only twice a year. You can take it in several locations across the world including Japan.

If your goal is to become an official ESL instructor, take the proper courses, get your credentials and apply to become a full-time teacher at an elementary, middle, or high school. Keep going this route and you may even become a full-time professor at a Japanese university. I've bumped into a couple of these people so it is possible to succeed in Japan going down this route.

How to break a lease

Now that the emotional work is out of the way, it's time to move. Breaking a lease and the method involved will depend largely on the contract you signed before you rented the apartment. For the sake of providing an example however, I will tell you my experience. To break my housing contract all I had to do was first email Relocation Japan (my middleman housing company) with a set time of when I was hoping to leave the country, my plan hoping to exit the apartment, and when to schedule utilities to be shutdown (gas, water, electricity) etc.

PRO TIP: I recommend you give yourself 48 hours or more to stay in a hotel leading to your departure from the country. The reason why is because things go wrong with inspections as they did with mine and the last thing you want is to be rushing an inspection and then you miss your flight because of poor planning. I gave myself four days in the hotel and while I was originally hoping to have the gas shutdown first since I could eat out, and then the water and electricity on the second day and the inspection on a 3rd day at night, March is apparently the time when everyone moves so the realtor could only do the inspection on a set day with every part taking place at once.

HEADS UP: Did I mention moving can be awful when you're trying to get rid of your garbage as well since certain garbage is only collected once a week? You might have to leave your garbage out for a week even after your inspection is over. The way to avoid this from happening is to basically get rid all of your garbage one week before the inspection. This means, with the exception of your bed or futon, everything should be out. (Desks, cutlery, etc.) Get it all out.

Disposing of furniture

Getting rid of plastic items, cardboard boxes, shoes, and other things are okay and easy to do on specific garbage collection days, but what about vacuum cleaners, refrigerators, televisions, sofas, futons, beds, desks etc.? You have three options.

Option A: Trade these items or sell them to incoming JETs. Use Craig's List, Facebook, or any other resource you can use to sell your items. Obviously if you've rented these items, the rental company will pick them up. If you're leaving early you may have a hard time and might need to rely on options B and C.

Option B: Discard these items as *sōdaigomi* 粗大ごみ(large trash) and have the city dispose of them cheaply. Every ward has a *sōdaigomi* service provided by the ward office. To contact your office, type into Google the name of your city in Japanese and the word 区役所 *kuyakusho* and 粗大 ごみ. If you don't understand, get a friend to help translate.

Next since these websites sometimes don't record the data correctly, I suggest you call the ward office and negotiate the deal. (See this is why it pays to learn Japanese before you go and while you're in Japan. You can take care of things much faster). Call the ward office and tell them what you need picked up and they will then tell you how many stickers you need. These stickers are a part of the disposal system and categorize items by size and weight so the ward office can prepare the appropriate transportation to remove unwanted furniture. When you call the ward office they will tell you exactly how many category A, B, and C stickers you will need from your local convenience store. The stickers cost anywhere from $2.00 - $4.00 per sticker, so write down what you told them you wanted to toss (maximum of 10 items per trip) and the stickers required. Any objects you did not mention or if you put the wrong sticker on the object will cause the garbage services to leave the item. You will need to write the date, your service number as provided by the ward office over the phone, and your name.

Stickers needed for disposing furniture. You can get these at your convenience store.

If you're still working during this time like I was since I needed the money for March, you may have to pull out these items at night so they're disposed of while you're at work. Doing this in a rainstorm at night in March sucks. Take it from me personally. Look ahead on your ward office's garbage service's website to see which days in the month they are doing large garbage pickup runs and plan accordingly. I recommend a good five to six weeks to get all of this organized if you want to get out without experiencing any hardship.

Option C: The super quick, but most expensive option is to call any contract garbage company to haul your furniture and recycle it. They will come even at night, but they will charge you up to $50.00 or more for certain items. These guys are also known to bait and switch, so be sure you're reading the websites correctly and their fine print. I had to hold on to items due to the ridiculous prices these guys were demanding at the last minute. Thankfully, I negotiated they take away the fridge and washing machine for a combined total of $30.00, so it wasn't entirely bad, but still frustrating.

Inspections

So once the gas, electricity, water, and your Internet services have been disconnected and you have visited the ward office and told them you are leaving the country, all that remains is the inspection. For this inspection you need to do a few other things.

1) All items including suitcases must be outside the apartment. Everything should be out and if you've done it correctly, nothing should be inside the apartment but you.
2) Everything must be vacuumed and cleaned. The realtors will charge a $300.00 cleaning fee, which is stupid in my opinion, but they can also charge you extra if areas are dirty which they will do and take it out of your deposit which you're supposed to get back. Do your part and clean.
3) Clean the walls by taking a cloth and wiping dirt or dust away.

Inspection scams, a $500 conversation

Realtors have a bad reputation in Japan. I've dealt with dozens of them. Whether they are trying to sell you property or inspecting it, they are infamous in the country for trying to rob people. Here's what happened to me. I had the inspector come in and explain everything to me in 100% Japanese. Here's the issue, had I not understood Japanese, I would've probably lost $500.00. Since I was leaving early, the realtor could only charge me for the days I was staying in the apartment, ideally five days in March. This inspector tried to con me by saying that even if I was leaving early in March, I had to pay an entire month's worth of rent. Relocation Japan knew I was skeptical of realtors and offered to provide support over the phone should I run into hiccups. What should've been a 20-minute inspection, turned into an hour and 10-minute inspection negotiating prices. Relocation Japan told the inspector he was misinformed, so I got my money.

However, the inspector didn't give up and dinged me for having an outline of dust on the wall where my desk and computer was and charged me $150.00 and threatened to press charges for damages should I attempt to clean it in front of him. As you can imagine, this inspector was really making me start to hate Japanese people, but I swallowed my anger and pressed on. He tried to ding me again since I forgot to uninstall a light bulb in the ceiling and he said he would charge me an additional $30.00 if I left it. I said fine, I took it from his hands and proceeded to walk outside towards my suitcases. Once he realized he was being a jerk for his behavior towards someone just trying to leave the country, he apologized for his behavior with everything and admitted that his recent behavior towards me was unprofessional. He took the light fixture and said his company could use it for their office and he agreed not to charge me and we even quoted it to Relocation Japan so I wouldn't get charged.

My point: You had better clean every speck of dust and be prepared for an absolute jerk of an inspector. Be prepared to argue in Japanese like I did, and if you lack the necessary skills, get one of your teachers or Japanese friends to go to bat for you. The middleman housing company provided by JET can help, but I hope none of you have to experience what I went through alone. I sort of won, I'd say out of the four debates we had I only lost one so that's not bad, but still had I not known Japanese I would have lost hundreds of dollars within a single afternoon.

Sending your luggage ahead to the airport

Some of the airports in Japan will allow you to have the airport pick up your luggage at your residence in Japan and store it at the airport up to the day you depart. Usually Japanese airports will store luggage for 2-3 days. This service really helped me when I was bringing back three suitcases and didn't want to haul them all the way to the airport with my friends who were seeing me off. The price is around $20.00 a suitcase, but will vary depending on the weight and size or your bag. For more detailed information including where you would pick up your bags visit: https://www.narita-airport.jp/en/service/svc_05 (this is Narita Airport's pickup service).

HEADS UP: I had trouble having the airport service come to my apartment since I was at work up to the day before I returned home. So I used the hotel I was staying at in my final few days handle the pickup service for me and arrange all of the details. It all worked out in the end, but keep in mind you may have to negotiate with your hotel staff if you're not living in an apartment during your final days in Japan.

Closing your bank account

To close your bank account you will need to do a few things. First you need to call them ahead of time and explain that you are leaving the country and would like to transfer all funds to your US account. Banks in Japan these days have an English support hotline you can call, so they should be able to walk you through the process. Once the funds have been transferred, you need to safely return to your home country and call the company (using Skype or another online call service) and tell them you wish to close the account. Some banks will allow you to even keep the account for free in the event you decide to visit Japan, but otherwise you are legally required to shut down the account. Once you finish that call, your account should be closed.

Pension

All JETs are entitled to a pension that reflects how long they have worked in Japan. Whether you work for one year or longer, you will get a pension after you return home to the United States and forfeit your Japanese visa. In order to receive your pension, you need to do a few things. First you need to fill out the application form, and get your blue pension book with you and leave the country. (*see photo below*). Also make sure you have a Japanese native be your tax identifier so you can apply for taxes and get your money back, 20% if I recall correctly. Be sure you've registered the change of address at your ward office and state that you're leaving the country. When you leave Japan, the immigration officer at the airport punches a hole through your ID card symbolizing you've left.

Then you need to fill out another set of forms, submit a copy of your passport with the legal permit stating that you were in an instructor, your blue book, and the application forms. Wait a few months and you should receive a deposit in your bank account. You have up to two years to apply for your pension so get cracking on it. It usually takes four to six months to process.

Photo of your blue payment book needed for your pension application.

Conclusion

Working for the JET Program is a huge honor and an amazing opportunity for physical and spiritual growth. You're exposed to Japan for more than a year and you get the chance to leave a cultural impact on those you meet. I really enjoyed the JET program. It provided me time to study the language, make new friends, immerse myself in a foreign environment, and figure out what I wanted in life. Everyone's experience is different, but I hope you walk away from the program refreshed and proud that you've grown and made a positive impact on several people during your stay. The memories you've made there will last a lifetime and I hope you can share them with your loved ones and children.

For further questions on the JET program, you can contact me at adamtheole@gmail.com

Good luck and I hope this guide serves you well.

Made in the USA
Columbia, SC
28 May 2023

17461613R00117